DURHAM

1000 years of history

For
Kate,
David, Mary and William
and
Those Who Watch Over

DURHAM

1000 years of history ✓

Martin Roberts

TEMPUS

First published 1994
This edition first published 2003

PUBLISHED IN THE UNITED KINGDOM BY:
Tempus Publishing Ltd
The Mill, Brimscombe Port
Stroud, Gloucestershire GL5 2QG

PUBLISHED IN THE UNITED STATES OF AMERICA BY:
Tempus Publishing Inc.
2 Cumberland Street
Charleston, SC 29401

British Library Cataloguing in Publication Data.
A catalogue record for this book is available from the British Library.

ISBN 0 7524 2537 4

Typesetting and origination by Tempus Publishing.
Printed in Great Britain by Midway Colour Print, Wiltshire.

CONTENTS

ACKNOWLEDGEMENTS
TO THE FIRST EDITION (1993)

Since coming to Durham almost twenty years ago I have been fortunate in learning about this wonderful city from a great many people, whose enthusiasm and knowledge I have invariably found infectious and absorbing. Several of them kindly helped me with information for, and the preparation of, this book, and to them I am particularly grateful. My thanks to Mr Bev Bagnall, Dr Richard Brigstock, Mr David Butler, Dr Margaret Bonney, Dr Eric Cambridge, Wing-Commander Albert Cartmell, Mr Peter Clack, Professor Rosemary Cramp, Mrs June Crosby, Mr Ian Curry, Dr Ian Doyle, Mrs Linda Drury, Mr Norman Emery, Miss Margot Johnson, Mrs Jo Jones, Mr Dennis Jones, Mr Martin Leyland, Mrs Grace McCombie, Miss Dorothy Meade, Dr Martin Millett, Mr Pat Mussett, Mr Roger Norris, Mrs Dolly Potter, Mr Peter Ryder, Mr Tony Scott, Professor Michael Tooley, Mr Pat Warren, Mr Neville Whittaker, Mr Don Wilcock, Mr Jon Williams and Mr Pat Woodward.

In assembling material I have received generous help from the staffs of the Dean and Chapter Library, Durham Cathedral, Department of Palaeography and Diplomatic at the University of Durham, Durham University Library, Durham City Library and Durham County Record Office.

I am grateful to those individuals acknowledged in the text and captions, who have kindly allowed me to quote them or redraft their drawings. Thanks to Dr and Mrs J. Hawgood for permission to redraw the plan of Crook Hall and to the following architects for permission to redraw their plans: Ian Curry, HLB Architects, Stringer and Jones. The castle plan and a number of the church plans are based on drawings from the *Victoria County History of Durham*. All line drawings are by the author.

I acknowledge the kind permission of the following publishers to allow extracts from their books: Cambridge University press (*Lordship and the Urban Community* by Margaret Bonney), Penguin Books (*Buildings of England: County Durham* by Nikolaus Pevsner and Elizabeth Williamson) and Yale University Press (*Carolingian and Romanesque Architecture* by Kenneth John Conant).

Photographic credits are given with the captions. Special thanks to Royston Thomas, the City of Durham Council's Directorate of Technical Services and Economic Development Unit for the loan of photographs. Thanks to John

Jennings for assistance with illustrative material and especially to John Lines, Graeme Stearman, Claire Chapman and Building Control for much technical advice. Sue Jones kindly helped with indexing.

Much of my enthusiasm for Durham I have shared with colleagues in the City Planning Office, since 1974. Their dedication to the protection of this city, and their individual insights into its character have long gone unacknowledged. To them, my thanks.

The City of Durham Council, whose good record of conservation and environmental management is well known, gave me permission to write this book. It is a private undertaking and the views expressed are my own.

Finally I must thank my children, David, Mary and William for assistance with typing and printing, and especially my wife, Kate, who read the entire text and made many valuable comments upon it. All in all, a family effort.

ACKNOWLEDGEMENTS
TO THE SECOND EDITION

Since the original Batsford publication of this book in 1993, I have received kind comments and criticisms. Errors have been gently pointed out to me. For this new enlarged Tempus edition I have sought further advice from many of the friends and colleagues thanked in the first edition and others newly acknowledged here. I have also benefited from a further decade of debate about Durham's buildings. In addition to those mentioned above I must thank the Durham WEA 'Cottage to Castle' class, Niall Hammond, Fiona McDonald, Tracey Ingle, Chris Fish, Richard Annis, Margaret Maddison, Brian Cheesman and Katherine Beer for years of enjoyable discussion. I only regret that I can no longer benefit from the good advice of my friend, Don Wilcock, who died last year.

For help on the current edition I thank Douglas Pocock and Dorthy Meade for helpful comments. Adrian Green offered illuminating advice on post-Dissolution Durham, Richard Brigstock and especially Ian Doyle offered help with the history of the castle, while Norman Emery and Christopher Downs gave generously of their time in pointing out errors and new insights on the cathedral. John Pendlebury kindly allowed me to distil his excellent paper on the work of Thomas Sharp.

The photographic credits in the first edition carry forward and are noted in illustration captions. I would again thank Royston Thomas for the use of his superb photographs, and the City of Durham Council for the loan of a number of them. My son David kindly took some additional photographs.

The cross-checking and rereading of the enlarged chapters has again been undertaken by my wife Kate, and the whole text given a critical review and proof read by Sue Jones, for which very many thanks.

Permission to undertake this enlarged revision was given by my employer, English Heritage (North East Region). To my colleagues there, with their sharp perceptions of Durham and its buildings, I offer my thanks for over three years of stimulating and entertaining discussion on the city. However, the writing of this book is a personal and private undertaking and the views expressed are my own.

A serious omission of the first edition was the thanks due to Peter Kemmis Betty, then Publishing Director of B.T. Batsford. Peter, now Group Publishing

Director of Tempus Publishing, approached me about this new edition and has continued to guide me through the mysteries of publication with his usual wisdom and good humour. Many thanks to him and to his colleagues Tim Clarke, and especially Emma Parkin.

Finally a word about this new enlarged edition. Errors and factual updates have been addressed I hope. The extra text has allowed me to develop some topics only briefly mentioned originally and to report on some of the new research in the past decade. I have been able to highlight areas where Durham may lay claim to a special contribution in the field of architectural history and finally I have indulged a little in buildings that hold a deep personal interest for me.

The rewrite has also found me asking more questions than may have been apparent in the first edition. A popular book on architectural history must try to meet the demands of some readers wanting simple facts with those wanting more discerning analysis – this balance has often been hard to achieve. So if this edition seems to raise more doubts, seems less surefooted than it was ten years ago, I hope all readers will see that as a sign of maturity! Often with an increase in knowledge comes a decrease in certainty – 'the more you know, the less you know'. I hope this book will at least be seen as a testament to the irrepressible fascination that this great city can engender. Durham still weaves its magic.

Old Fleece House, West Auckland
November 2002

PREFACE

The approach to Whinney Hill is very special. You climb on its eastern side, blind to the town, towards a stand of six trees starkly silhouetted on the horizon. As you rise, so Durham rises too. First framed in the trees, then spreading out across the whole skyline – cathedral, castle and town. In a city of many wonderful experiences, Whinney Hill is particularly memorable. It makes you catch your breath.

In the summer of 1665 an artist, Bok, of whom we know little, stood on that same summit and drew the same panorama of cathedral, castle and town – a sketch later engraved and now kept in the Bodleian Library in Oxford. His sketch is generally well set out and by matching foreground to background buildings, corner to corner, tower to pinnacle, it is easy to find the precise spot on which he stood and drew on that summer's day.

Bok's momentary sense of wonder, preserved in his sketch, binds him to the modern observer. And beyond them both is the nameless medieval pilgrim, who also stood on the hilltop and gave thanks for safe arrival at the Shrine of St Cuthbert. All three, though foreigners to each other, absorbed in their own time and culture, are kindred spirits. Their experience is the same . . . the catching of breath . . . that is beyond words.

What these three saw, looking down on the city, were the same constant symbols – cathedral, castle and town. But each was looking at buildings that had undergone countless changes of both function and fabric. It is the purpose of this book to explore how these buildings have developed over the centuries, to try to interpret and understand how Durham comes to look the way it does.

When I began to write this book I hoped to form some clear definition of 'Durham'. As work progressed new areas for research opened up, new contradictions needed explaining. In the end I have yielded to these irresistible centrifugal forces, content that 'Durham' defies universal classification. The reader will, like Bok and the nameless pilgrim before him, fashion his or her own personal experience of the city, bound together, in part at least, by that 'catching of breath'.

I hope you will enjoy this book, will share in its sense of exploration and will want to make discoveries of your own.

The city from Whinney Hill (**colour plate 1**), *Bok's view* (**6**)

1
OUTLINE HISTORY

Geology and geomorphology

Over 250 million years ago, the area of the present city of Durham lay beneath a vast primordial sea. The subsequent creation of the Pennine mountain range to the west folded and uplifted the bedrock, tilting it gently to the east. The city area lay within a wide belt of coal measure sandstone, in a broad valley at the confluence of two rivers, the Browney and the Wear (**colour plate 3**).

After the Ice Age, the area again found itself underwater in a large lake of glacial melt waters dammed by the receding ice flow to the north. The glacial deposits choked the old river valleys at the junction of the Browney and Wear; the Browney was forced to turn south. Where the Wear reworked its old, drift-filled channels, wide flood plains developed. In contrast, where the river cut into solid rock to avoid the buried river valley, narrow steep-sided gorges were formed, nowhere more dramatically than in the meander around the peninsula at Durham (**1**).

Early man in Durham

Upon the settled post-glacial landscape, colonisation by herbaceous plants was followed about 10,000 years ago by gradual afforestation. Juniper first, then birch, hazel and pine, followed by elm and oak.

Man's first appearance in the city area must have been as the nomadic hunter of the Palaeolithic and Mesolithic periods, which ended *c.*4000 BC, but few permanent imprints were left. The landscape of the area at this time was densely wooded, except where the river flowed through reed swamps in the shallow valleys of the glacial drift. The Neolithic and Bronze Age peoples, 3000-700 BC, settled in the area and gradually deforestation began. This took the form of small-scale clearance, intensive and exhaustive farming of the land, abandonment and new clearance.

During the Iron Age, 700 BC to AD 70, more settlements in the Wear lowlands were established and over 30 have been recorded within a 15km (9 mile) radius of Durham. Closer to the city lies Maiden Castle, an Iron Age hill

1 *The Wear gorge below St Oswald's, where the churchyard prevented quarrying for building stone in the medieval period, so preserving the original steep cliff face.* Royston Thomas

fort, once moated by the River Wear on three sides, and needing only a deep ditch on its western flank to complete its defences. Opposite, on the banks of the Wear's flood plain, a farmstead was established at Old Durham, a little to the south of the farm hamlet that bears its name today. Scant finds on the peninsula itself may point to a similar settlement there too, with its attendant forest clearance (**2**).

Roman Durham

Roman roads approached Durham from three directions, but their routes through the city are unknown. The military road, Dere Street, *c.*AD 78-84, away to the west, headed northwards to Hadrian's Wall. The route of the later Cade's Road through the city may have passed Old Durham northwards, crossing the Wear near Kepier. Its line has not been found, nor that of a link road from Dere Street, approaching from the south west (**2**).

2 *Map of pre-995 Durham, showing the known early settlements at Maiden Castle (1) and Old Durham (2), as well as the location of prehistoric finds (crosses) and Roman finds (dots). These are overlaid on the geological map of the area, indicating the sandstone outcrops (stippled) and the pre-glacial river valleys*

What is known is the Romanisation, during the second and fourth centuries AD, of the native farmstead at Old Durham originally established by the indigenous population. A bath–house, together with circular threshing floors, was discovered here during gravel workings in the 1940s. On the peninsula the earliest finds from the third quarter of the first century AD suggest, as at Old Durham, the Romanisation of a native farm rather than any military presence. There is a general suspicion amongst local historians and archaeologists that the peninsula at Durham was too good a site not to be occupied in some form in the years before the arrival of the Community of St Cuthbert. The substantial physical evidence for that settlement has yet to be discovered.

Anglo-Saxon Northumbria

With the departure of the Romans in the early fifth century, there followed a period of invasion and settlement by the Anglo-Saxons. The small tribes that settled in the region formed two powerful groupings, the Deirans and the Bernicians, later allied by royal marriage. They subjugated the native Britons and Celts and formed the kingdom of Northumbria. The growth of the kingdom in the early seventh century is marked by two waves of missionary activity: St Paulinus of the Roman church arrived in York c.627 and St Aidan established his Celtic mission from Iona, on Lindisfarne in 635. The conflict over the traditions of these two churches was resolved in favour of the Roman church at the Synod of Whitby in 664. The subsequent fusion of Celtic, Anglo-Saxon and Roman culture led to a flowering of Anglo-Saxon art, centred on the monasteries of Lindisfarne, Monkwearmouth (founded 674) and Jarrow (681).

During this period we know nothing of Durham. Forest clearance would have continued around the native settlements, especially along the banks of the Wear's flood plain where cultivation would have been most productive. The first possible documented date for a settlement at Durham comes in the *Anglo-Saxon Chronicles*. In 762, Peohtwine was consecrated Bishop of Whithorn in Galloway, at a place called *Aelfet ee* or Aelfet Island. Claims have been made for the settlement being Elvet at Durham, centred around the church of St Oswald (2). These have yet to be proved and no archaeological evidence has been found to substantiate them.

The Community of St Cuthbert

Around the year 995, the central event in the history of the city took place – the Community of St Cuthbert arrived on the Durham peninsula bearing the body of their saint. Around the saintliness of his life and the incorruptibility of his body in death, there grew up a wealth of truths, half-truths, myths and legends. Cuthbert became the subject of a powerful propagandist tradition, sustained for both political and economic reasons. He was born in the Scottish borders a little before 635, and around his sixteenth birthday he entered the monastery at Melrose under Abbot Eata, later his mentor and patron. In 664, after the Synod of Whitby, Eata and Cuthbert transferred to Lindisfarne as abbot and prior respectively. In 678 Eata was made Bishop of Lindisfarne and seven years later Cuthbert succeeded him. His acceptance of this high office was reluctant and shortly before his death in 687, as Bede tells us, he 'threw aside the burden of his pastoral care and determined to return to the strife of a hermit's life that he loved so well'.

The cult of St Cuthbert developed swiftly after his death, accelerated by the discovery in 698 of his incorrupt body. Pilgrims flocked to the newly elevated relics in his shrine. In 793 Lindisfarne suffered from the first Viking raid and in the decades that followed the Community in the monastery felt increasingly insecure. After further raids in 875, they decided to leave, taking with them the body of their saint. Eight years of wandering ended at Chester-le-Street, where the Community settled until 995. Once again raids forced a move south to Ripon. After four months they left to return north.

The delightful tale of the Community's arrival at Durham, involving an immovable cart which bore St Cuthbert's coffin, was faithfully chronicled by Symeon, a twelfth-century monk from Durham. Later writers added the even more colourful stories of cowgirls and lost cows. Sadly the reality was much less miraculous and more calculating. The Community's leader, Bishop Aldhun, like many Saxon priests, was married. In offering his daughter's hand to Uchtred, later Earl of Northumbria, he was dowered with extensive lands for the church. In seeking a permanent home for the Community, the ideal situation was within those lands, which were under Uchtred's protection, in a well-fortified site that was also sufficiently isolated to preserve and defend resources. For Uchtred the new foundation would represent the establishment of an impregnable fortress from which to resist Danes and Scots, while harnessing the power and reputation of St Cuthbert to his cause of 'Northumbrian separatism'.

The Community of St Cuthbert at Durham

According to Symeon, on reaching Durham in 995 the Community found the peninsula covered with dense woodland 'with the sole exception of a moderate sized plain . . . kept under cultivation having been regularly ploughed and sown'. This pre-monastic presence may refer to either the survival of an earlier native settlement or the work necessary to fortify and prepare the ground prior to the Community's arrival. Before moving onto the peninsula, the

17

Community may have stayed in the church of St Oswald in nearby Elvet. The discovery of a fine Anglo-Saxon cross with somewhat archaic decoration, buried in the church walls, has led to the suggestion that it was erected by the monks to mark the saint's rest here, and executed in a style deliberately evocative of their Lindisfarne origins.

Once on the peninsula they erected a temporary shelter for the saint's body while a further timber church, the *Alba Ecclesia,* was built, which remained in use until the consecration of the great stone church, the *Ecclesia Major,* in 998. For the construction of this church, Uchtred pressed the local populace 'from the Coquet to the Tees' into the work. The conveniently miraculous cure of a crippled woman had, meantime, reaffirmed the power of the Cuthbertine pilgrimage and the influence of the city began to spread. Evidence of fortifications at this time is circumstantial, though any walls or palisades would doubtless have been strengthened following renewed Danish activity early in the eleventh century. In the same period the Scots twice besieged the city and twice suffered defeat and dreadful slaughter. As its reputation grew as both a place of pilgrimage and an impregnable fortress, Durham became the focus of northern resistance against the new conquerors – the Normans.

The Normans

William the Conqueror's hold on his new kingdom was always fragile in the years immediately after 1066, particularly in the north where his chosen Earls of Northumbria were twice murdered. When the new appointee rebelled, William's patience broke. He dispatched Robert Cumin north, as the new earl, at the head of a large army. On 30 January 1069 Cumin entered Durham with 700 men. The next day the English poured into the city and slew the Normans. Cumin perished when his house was set on fire, the blaze almost spreading to the western tower of the Anglo-Saxon cathedral nearby. The revolt spread south into Yorkshire. William again responded, with the so-called 'harrying of the north', the systematic destruction of humans, animals and property as far as the Tees. In Durham, the Community feared reprisals and fled north to Lindisfarne, returning early in 1070. When the new Norman bishop, Walcher, was murdered in 1080, William dispatched Bishop Odo of Bayeux, whose army was garrisoned at Durham, to carry out the ravaging of Northumbria.

In 1083, Walcher's successor, St Calais (1080-96) introduced the Benedictine monastic rule to Durham, replacing the old Community with monks from Jarrow, and subsequently divided the palatinate estates to endow the new priory. In 1088 he unwisely supported Odo in rebellion against the king, William II, but received only a lenient sentence of three years exile in Normandy. Returning in 1091, his castle and see restored, St Calais was also

3 *The castle and cathedral from the north-west at Framwellgate. Flambard's extensive building works on the peninsula were complemented by his development of the Bishop's Borough on both sides of the River Wear, linked by Framwellgate Bridge. First built around 1120, the bridge was rebuilt in the early fifteenth century.* City of Durham Council

enriched by the great gifts he had received. This new wealth enabled him to undertake his crowning achievement, the building of the great Romanesque cathedral church, begun in 1093. When St Calais died in 1096, William II kept the see vacant for over three years before appointing his most powerful minister, Ranulf Flambard, as bishop (1099-1128). Described as 'an energetic and picturesque ruffian, whose wickedness astounded the medieval chroniclers', Flambard nonetheless made a great impact on Durham, undertaking major building work in the cathedral, castle and town (**3**). At his death in 1128, the see remained vacant, during which time the priory again financed work on the cathedral.

The episcopates of Bishops Geoffrey Rufus and William of St Barbara in the middle of the twelfth century marked a period of great turmoil in the history of Durham, reflecting the miserable state of the whole country during the anarchy of King Stephen's reign. Stephen's rival for the throne, the Empress Matilda, had a great champion in her uncle, King David I of Scotland, who invaded England in 1136 and progressed to the outskirts of Durham, until halted by Stephen's army. A renewed Scottish assault in 1138 was crushed at the Battle of the Standard, after which David sued for peace. In the Treaty of Durham, concluded the following year, Stephen bought off his northern opponent with very favourable terms, granting him the earldom of Northumberland. The bishopric's Cuthbertine territories within the earldom remained independent – 'an oasis in a Scottish Northumbria'.

In 1141, during the brief ascendancy of Matilda to the English throne, David claimed the vacant see for his chancellor, William Cumin, thereby annexing the bishopric. Cumin occupied the castle, but a band of monks escaped to York to elect William of St Barbara as bishop. St Barbara raised an army to oppose Cumin and pitched camp at Gilesgate. Cumin, in reprisal, devastated the cathedral and later Elvet and Gilesgate. Only in 1144 did St Barbara regain his see, aided by the Earl of Northumberland. The northern counties were finally returned to England under Henry II in 1157.

Hugh of Le Puiset

When St Barbara died in 1152, Durham lay a damaged city in a Scottish enclave. The desperate times emboldened the monks to choose as their new bishop the youthful Hugh of Le Puiset, an able administrator, treasurer of York and the King's nephew. Scarcely a religious man – he had fathered three children – he offered a firm hand and strong government. The early part of his episcopate was pre-occupied with disputes with the King, but later his aspirations and achievements as the supreme territorial lord in the north of England blossomed in a great building programme that, like that of his predecessor Flambard, embraced the whole city. In 1179 Le Puiset granted a charter to the growing Bishop's Borough to the north of the castle, allowing the burgesses specific liberties and customs. It marked the culmination of the growth of the city begun almost 200 years before. Durham became a major pilgrimage centre, and an active, if modest, trading and market town.

From his capital city, the Bishop of Durham exerted great authority – he could appoint civil officers, exercise jurisdiction, raise armies and mint his own coins. The power base of the quasi-regal 'Prince Bishops' had been established that was to endure throughout the medieval period (**colour plate 2**).

Reginald – chronicler of Durham

Le Puiset's achievements in both the city and the wider Palatinate have been recorded in documents of the period. In 1183, the Boldon Book was drawn up giving a detailed picture of all the bishop's lands, listing tenants, their land holdings and tenurial duties. Sadly, on Durham it is largely silent. Fortunately, this is not the case for two books written by Reginald, one of Le Puiset's monks. The first concerns the miracles of St Cuthbert, the second is a life of St Godric, the famous recluse of nearby Finchale. From both books it is possible to draw many references to the city in Le Puiset's time.

Outside the city, mention is made of Kepier and the church of St Giles and beside the *via regia*, probably the old route to Newcastle, a cross stood about a mile from the city. This may have been one of the circle of crosses around the town marking a boundary on the approach to the sanctuary of Durham Cathedral, of which only the Neville's and Charley Crosses survive in fragments. Within the walled city, Reginald describes the cathedral and parish churches, the lodging houses for pilgrims, the market stalls and open-fronted shops along the streets, and the muddy approach to the cathedral. From near here he glanced across the river gorge to see the white-fronted houses of South Street, much as one can see them today, on emerging from Windy Gap.

Throughout his writings Reginald remarks upon the crowds in Durham, pilgrims to the shrine, and his book serves as a powerful testament to the success − religious, political and economic − that the cult of St Cuthbert brought to the town.

The thirteenth century

When Le Puiset died in 1195, lesser men followed who spent much of their time protecting the great powers won for them by their Norman predecessors. To settle the growing rift between bishop and priory, a *Convenit* was signed in 1229, which defined the two great estates and their spheres of influence. Anthony Bek became bishop in 1284 and though more powerful than his predecessors, was much distracted by attempts both by the King and the priory to erode his power base. Despite the preoccupations of respective bishops, the century saw major works to both the cathedral and castle.

The Scottish threat

The King who had challenged Bek was Edward I, the 'Hammer of the Scots'. Edward never accepted the equality and independence of a neighbouring kingdom in Scotland, and the Scottish treaty with France in 1295, shortly after the outbreak of Anglo-French hostilities, was the last straw. Edward's army moved through Durham the following year on its way to victory at Dunbar. Two years later the Wallace revolt was crushed.

By 1307 fortunes were reversed with the accession of the weak Edward II matched by the rise of the energetic and ambitious Scottish king, Robert Bruce, who led raids into England. In the year of Bek's death in 1311, the new bishop, Kellaw, excused himself from the Court of Rome because of the Scottish attacks on the city. This prophetic action anticipated the long years of conflict that were to follow. The Scots attacked the city again in 1313 and, emboldened by their total victory over Edward at Bannockburn the following year, they returned in 1315 before the townspeople in the Market Place could

4 *Neville's Cross was one of a series of crosses on the approaches to the medieval city which may have marked significant steps in the approach to the sanctuary in Durham Cathedral. The cross was already standing and named when the great battle of 1346 took place. It was rebuilt by Ralph Neville after the battle. This reconstruction by the author is based upon a description of it in* The Rites of Durham *and contemporary examples*

put up the wall granted them by the bishop. This disastrous decade for the city was further compounded by famine (1313) and flooding (1315).

An Anglo-Scottish truce of 1319 was broken by English attacks in 1322, countered by a Scottish raid deep into Yorkshire. A further truce the following year was broken by a Scottish attack into Weardale in 1327. A truce of 1328 was broken in 1332, after which the peace of 1334 was followed by more war and the gradual erosion of English control of southern Scotland as Edward III looked towards France in pursuit of his ambitions. The Scottish revival only ended when David II of Scotland led his army south in 1346 to divert the English army from their French military campaign. In the western outskirts of the city, at Nevilles Cross, he was intercepted by the northern barons, his army decimated and the King himself captured.(**4**)

Why this litany of historical events in a book about buildings and land-scapes? Medieval Durham was a border town. Hence relations between England and Scotland were always central to its history and development. In the first half of the fourteenth century, specifically 1296-1346, the threat or the reality of a Scottish attack was almost continually present. The reinforcement of the Northgate in 1313, the recutting of the castle's inner moat and the 'stable-door' construction of the town wall after 1315 are all direct military responses, reflected throughout Northumbria in towns, castles and fortified buildings. Can subtler evidence be found elsewhere in the city?

Crook Hall was rebuilt in this period on its isolated and undefended site. Are its old-fashioned narrow lancets just northern conservatism or are they defensive? Was its incomplete moat abandoned on the signing of a new truce or the final defeat of 1346? The Kepier gatehouse of 1341-5 may well be a peacetime rebuilding of part of the hospital destroyed in earlier Scottish raids, although the hospital also suffered an unrelated fire in 1306, which might explain the new work. The collective mindset of Durham citizens in this period must have been sharply focussed on events to the north and this may well have found more physical forms as yet undiscovered.

The later medieval city

No sooner was the Scottish threat removed than Durham fell victim to the Black Death in 1349-50 and, in the century that followed, an economic depression afflicted the area, weakened by subsequent attacks of the plague in 1416 and 1438. The bishops were forced to lower their lease rentals and by 1446 tenements in the Baileys were wasted and decayed. Only in the latter half of the fifteenth century did the monastic economy recover.

Late medieval Durham was no longer the scene of major border warfare. It had settled into a quieter existence as a medium-sized urban community. If its market function reflected the traditional pattern of English medieval towns, then its servicing of the great institutions of the bishopric and the monastery was more unusual. The lack of any strong merchant elite in Durham was replaced by a professional hierarchy of administrators and officials owing fealty to their religious masters on the peninsula (**5**).

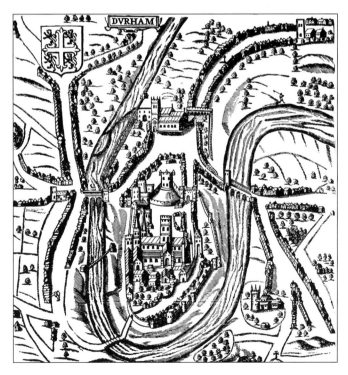

5 *Speed's 'Plan of Durham' is one of the earliest representations of the city. The cathedral is shown with its western spires, within the walled castle enclosure. At the southern end of the peninsula is the first wooden Prebends Bridge of 1574, rebuilt in stone in 1696 and finally replaced by the third Prebends Bridge in 1778, a little further downstream*

Tudor Durham

In 1494, nine years after the triumph of Henry Tudor (Henry VII) at Bosworth, Richard Fox became Bishop of Durham. As Secretary to the King, and later Keeper of the Privy Seal, Fox was an important figure at the Tudor court. He was entrusted by the King to negotiate the marriage of his daughter, Margaret, to the Scottish King James IV and, as Bishop of Winchester, Fox escorted her north to the ceremony in 1503, stopping at Durham where huge celebrations were held in the castle. Peace was short-lived, for in 1513 the Scots, angered at Henry VII's campaign in France, poured over the border into the bishopric, only to be crushed at the Battle of Flodden. In triumph, the banner of the dead Scottish King was hung over St Cuthbert's Shrine in the cathedral.

When Henry VIII assumed the title of Supreme Head of the Church of England in 1534, the unique privileges enjoyed by the Durham bishops posed a threat. In 1536 many of these powers were transferred to the King with the bishop, Cuthbert Tunstall, offering little resistance to the process. The same year saw the major county families, including the Nevilles, Bowes and Tempests, play their part in the Pilgrimage of Grace. This great revolt in the north of England, ignited by the suppression of the monasteries, was motivated by a wide range of issues, notably the centralisation of power and the new economic conditions. It was a cry against the passing of the old order and once it was crushed, Henry re-empowered the Council of the North, under Tunstall as President, to administer and control the rebellious region.

In March 1538, the King's Commissioners entered the monastic precincts of the cathedral and defaced the Shrine of St Cuthbert. This singular act was a catastrophe for the city's religious and economic life, it was the moment 'the very centre of the arch upholding the fabric of medieval Durham at once fell in'.

At the end of 1539 the monastery at Durham was surrendered to the king. It was to be re-established on a secular basis and in 1541 the last prior of the old monastery, Hugh Whitehead, became the first dean, twelve former monks becoming the first prebendaries or residentiary canons. Little physical damage was done to the cathedral during Whitehead's term of office, but his two successors, Robert Horne and William Whittingham, were great reformers. They smashed the stained glass and destroyed carvings and memorial stones including the statues of the Neville Screen.

The local population had little stomach for these reforms and dissatisfaction for the new order led to the Rising of the North in 1569. The Earls of Northumberland and Westmorland led a force from Raby Castle to Durham, where the old mass was restored at the cathedral. Despite the support of the populace, they failed to secure the release of Mary, Queen of Scots and received none of the expected Spanish assistance through the port of Hartlepool. In retreat, the earls were defeated north of Durham and fled to Scotland; their estates were forfeited to the crown and over five hundred of

their followers executed. The consequent impoverishment of the local aristoc-
racy only worsened the living standards of the general population who were
reduced to the verge of starvation.

In Durham, the Earl of Westmorland lost his town house in the Market
Place which was acquired by the newly-formed Corporation of Durham
(1565). This reform, introduced by Bishop Pilkington, created a civic body of
twelve men, who bore office only for as long as the Bishop saw fit.
Subservience was total, but the foundations of civic power had at least been laid.

The long reign of Elizabeth brought little benefit to Durham. The mistrust
and suspicion created by the northern rebellion convinced many at Elizabeth's
court that the north was a hotbed of barely concealed Catholicism. Nor could
the city avoid natural disasters. Crop failure in 1587 was followed two years
later by plague. This returned in 1597-9, over four hundred dying in Elvet
alone. Such catastrophic events should be set against the quieter records of
everyday life in the city. The state of Durham from the Dissolution to the
Restoration has often been portrayed as one of unremitting decline, countered
by a spectacular post-Restoration revival. The evidence of craftsmen's records,
churchwardens' accounts, Dean and Chapter rentals, etc. does indicate that the
physical fabric of the city was maintained. There was piecemeal rebuilding by
the more prosperous households, especially on the peninsula and around the
Market Place, while the parish churches were generally kept in good repair.

Nevertheless the economic outlook was still bleak and in 1602, in an effort
to reinvigorate a city suffering from disease and declining trade, Bishop
Matthew awarded a new civic charter free from episcopal interference. In so
doing he presaged the dispute between bishop and corporation that was to
figure so prominently in the rest of the century.

The seventeenth century

If the Tudors cared little for the rebellious and untrustworthy north, under the
Stuarts the area began to prosper. On one of the frequent royal visits, in 1617,
the townspeople petitioned James I to help them in 'this dull cell of earth
wherein we live'. Trade was stagnant but as the century progressed, the
influence of the old order of gentry families gave way to the new money from
the Newcastle coal owners, who were now investing in the county. To this
modest revival can be added the evidence of rebuilding in the city between
1600 and 1640, undertaken by the county gentry, palatine lawyers, medical
doctors and the clergy.

The bishops continued their relentless struggle to protect their episcopal
rights from the crown. At least as Lord Lieutenants of the Council of the
North, the bishops were able to discharge the king's military power as well as
their own jurisdictional and ecclesiastical authority. The submission of the

rights to the King only stiffened the resolve of the bishops to resist erosion of their powers within the city. They restricted the corporation's powers and denied the city any parliamentary representation.

At the outbreak of the Civil War, the ruling hierarchy and general populace of the county were of Royalist persuasion, but in the city the townspeople had some Parliamentary sympathies. When, during the earlier Bishops' Wars, the Scots occupied the city in 1640, they destroyed the cathedral's font and organ, and exacted financial payments from the citizens. The relief at their departure in 1641 was short-lived as they reoccupied the city three years later, an invasion aggravated by the return of bubonic plague.

The Interregnum of the Commonwealth and Protectorate period greatly benefited the citizens of Durham at the cost of the bishop. The bishopric was abolished, the dean and chapter suppressed and all church lands were put up for sale, including the castle. The corporation's rights were restored and parliamentary representation finally achieved. The cathedral, already damaged in two Scottish invasions, may well have suffered further assault during its occu-

pation in 1650 by 3,000 Scottish prisoners, captured by Cromwell at the Battle of Dunbar. In the same year moves were made to establish a college in the abandoned prebends' houses but, with the collapse of the Republic and the Restoration of Charles II, little was achieved.

The return of prebend John Cosin as bishop (1660-72) signalled a great revival in the physical wellbeing of the city. Campaigns of restoration in the castle and cathedral were reflected in general improvements throughout the town (**6**). Cosin's return was a mixed blessing to the local populace, who witnessed the dismantling of the democratic reforms achieved during the Interregnum and a return to the supremacy of the bishop in local politics. But the sale of crown and church lands had made land and property tenancies

6 *Bok's panorama of Durham from Whinney Hill (c.1665). Central portion showing St Oswald's (left foreground), the cathedral and castle within the peninsula walls, and Elvethall Manor (right foreground) on Hallgarth Street. Within the castle, Bishop Cosin's hall and staircase improvements are complete, but his terraced motte is still to be undertaken.* Bodleian Library, University of Oxford, Gough Maps 7, fol. 2b

uncertain during the Interregnum and a return to the old order, with its familiar repressions, was perhaps a price they were willing, if not content, to pay for stability. Bishop Crewe, who succeeded Cosin, was far more munificent, restoring both civic rights and parliamentary representation to the city.

Eighteenth and nineteenth centuries

The historical focus of the palatinate that in medieval times had so sharply focussed upon the city had, by the eighteenth century, moved away and was now more diffused across the whole county. The birth of rail transport and the development of the most productive coalfield in Victorian England took place elsewhere, leaving the city unaffected directly by the industrial expansion of the age. If the coal under the city was too thin to be mined on a large scale, Durham's position in the heart of the coalfield led to the establishment of the Durham Miners' Association in the city in 1869. Their annual Miners' Gala, inaugurated in 1871, was to become the focal point for the celebration of the labour movement in Britain.

The city had attempted to establish other industries and in 1780 a woollen mill was established in Walkergate but soon switched to carpet manufacture, which developed into a major industry in the town. A cotton mill erected in 1796 on the edge of St Oswald's churchyard was less successful, being destroyed by fire in 1804. Mustard production had been associated with the city from the early eighteenth century when it was first ground commercially. Its production ceased towards the end of the next century, overtaken by a cheaper product. Organ building was also well established with several practitioners in the nineteenth century, of which only one, Harrison and Harrison, survives today.

Improvements to communications were proposed, most ambitiously the plan to make the Wear navigable up to Durham. Mooted since the late seventeenth century, the scheme was revised and amended, but finally abandoned with the arrival of rail transport over 150 years later. Despite the inauguration of the Stockton and Darlington Railway in 1825, it was another 19 years before Durham was connected into the expanding rail network. In 1857 the viaduct was constructed but it was not until 1872 that there was a direct link between Newcastle upon Tyne and London. Roads were undergoing gradual improvement and, to link the city to the new roads to the west, King Street (later North Road) was constructed in 1831 – the first major addition to the medieval street pattern.

These developments in the city stimulated only modest population growth in comparison to the rapid increases in the new industrial centres (**7**). From a population of around 2,000-3,000 people in 1635, the city had grown to only 7,500 in 1801 and 16,000 by 1901, as compared to Sunderland's tenfold

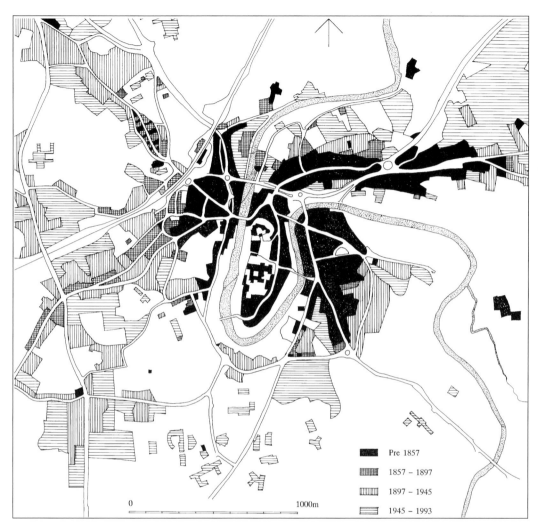

▇	Pre 1857
▦	1857 – 1897
▥	1897 – 1945
▤	1945 – 1993

0   1000m

7 *Durham has had to evolve within the varied landform of the area. The expansion, out from the peninsula, has avoided the low-lying flood plains of the River Wear to the north-east and south-east. Similarly many of its hilltops and valleys have not been built upon. The fragmented 'crab-like' plan of the city that resulted, with its close interplay of the built and natural environment, is one of its most distinctive characteristics*

increase during the nineteenth century. If the new wealth was not generated in the city, it often ended up there. For the industrial expansion on the restored church lands throughout the region had greatly benefited the cathedral authorities and the bishopric, and this found expression in many of the city's new developments. Most significant of these was the foundation of the university in 1832. It was created on the initiative and endowment of the dean and chapter, and the bishop, who relinquished his castle and moved permanently to Bishop Auckland.

The decade that had seen the birth of the university also saw the Municipal Reform Act of 1835. This established a new structure for local government in the city, abolished the rights and privileges enjoyed until then by the city guilds and removed the bishop from all involvement in civic affairs. The following year the temporal powers of the bishops of Durham in all matters were finally extinguished by their annexation to the crown.

Modern Durham

The growth of the university during the nineteenth century was modest, reflecting that of the town itself, and even into the twentieth century the population only rose by 3,000 to 19,000 between 1901 and 1921. The period between the First and Second World Wars was one of stagnation in Durham, caused by the Depression and the general decline in the county's basic heavy industries. Despite this lack of growth, the city underwent a number of important physical changes which saw it expand in all directions, out to the rim of its landscape bowl.

In the second half of the twentieth century, the city grew gradually and its subsequent history is essentially of local, and occasionally regional, importance. Its role in national affairs has never eclipsed its political and military significance under the Norman bishops, but the cultural importance of their inheritance, given to this small northern city, was brought sharply into focus by the designation of the cathedral and castle as a World Heritage Site in 1986.

2
THE CASTLE

Before all else Durham was a fortress. The long journey of the Community of St Cuthbert had begun because of their vulnerability to attack. What they found in Durham was a site naturally protected by the river gorge that, with relative ease, could be made fully secure. The weakness lay at the neck of the peninsula; and it is here that the first earth walls would have been raised, before the 'hill-island' was encircled with timber palisades. No firm evidence of the Saxon defences has yet been found.

Paradoxically, the first successful attack upon the fortress was made by the Saxons themselves when the Normans had occupied the town in 1069. It was the slaughter of William the Conqueror's army and the murder of his earl, Robert Cumin, that brought about the construction of the castle at Durham as a symbol of Norman power in the north and the re-establishment of William's regal authority.

The Norman castle-palace 1072-1217

The building of the castle was begun in 1072 by the new earl, Waltheof, at the instigation of King William. After his execution in 1076 the earldom was sold by the King to Bishop Walcher (1071-80) who began the construction of the principal ranges. The castle remained the principal residence of the bishops of Durham throughout the medieval period. The outer walls of the castle embraced the whole of the peninsula including the cathedral and priory, but the main defences were placed along its vulnerable northern boundary.

The Norman bishops of Durham from Walcher to Le Puiset faced two tasks in their building work at the castle. They were required by their master, the king, to maintain a fortress that would consolidate their hold on the region and defend it against both local rebellion and the Scottish nation to the north. They also needed to build a palace fit for one of the most powerful men in the north of England, a symbol of the quasi-regal powers the bishops enjoyed. Medieval palaces were not usually fortified, but the special responsibilities placed upon the bishops to defend the northern borders of the realm led to the construction of the castle-palace at Durham. Similar castle-palaces arose along the border with Wales, where Norman marcher lords also added splendid new buildings to their military fortresses.

The early work of the bishops of Durham in the north and west ranges of the castle gives a very rare glimpse into the architectural scale and lavishness of the palaces of Norman England. The royal palaces of the period have largely disappeared, though much can be deduced through excavation and archive research. At Durham, buildings of high quality still survive.

The chronology of the early Norman castle is still the subject of much debate and conjecture. Whether the motte or inner bailey was constructed first is unknown but, once the motte had stabilised, a timber tower was built on top, around which a stone ring wall was added later by Flambard (1099-1128). The inner bailey of the castle was constructed on its western flank while, on the east, the motte overlooked the main entry onto the peninsula through the North Gate (**8**). The inner bailey was enclosed by ranges of buildings on the north, east and west sides, with the gatehouse and perhaps other buildings to the south. The north wall was a free-standing structure of *c*.1072 before the

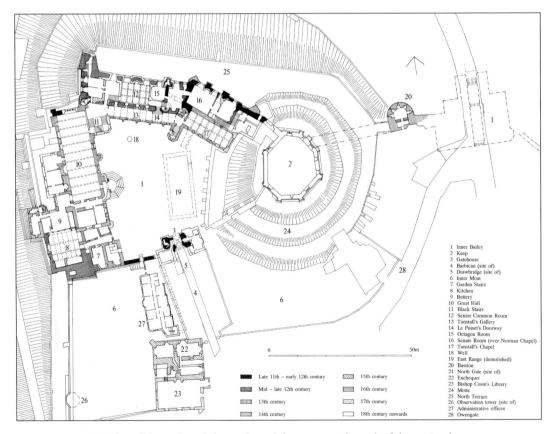

1	Inner Bailey
2	Keep
3	Gatehouse
4	Barbican (site of)
5	Drawbridge (site of)
6	Inner Moat
7	Garden Stairs
8	Kitchen
9	Buttery
10	Great Hall
11	Black Stairs
12	Senior Common Room
13	Tunstall's Gallery
14	Le Puiset's Doorway
15	Octagon Room
16	Senate Room (over Norman Chapel)
17	Tunstall's Chapel
18	Well
19	East Range (demolished)
20	Bastion
21	North Gate (site of)
22	Exchequer
23	Bishop Cosin's Library
24	Motte
25	North Terrace
26	Observation tower (site of)
27	Administrative offices
28	Owengate

Late 11th – early 12th century   15th century
Mid – late 12th century   16th century
13th century   17th century
14th century   18th century onwards

8 *Plan of the castle and the northern defences, across the neck of the peninsula*

building now known as the chapel was constructed against it, probably in the 1080s as part of a larger, two storey range.

This chapel is one of the most powerful expressions of early Norman architecture in the country (**colour plate 4**). The internal space is divided by two rows of three columns into 12 small groin-vaulted compartments, strongly suggesting it served as an undercroft for a first floor structure. It is built entirely of local sandstone, including its herringbone paving, an original feature. The circular columns have the most astonishing natural veining and are crowned with primitively sculpted capitals of energetic designs – flowers, leopards, stag hunting, human heads and, on one capital only, a Tau or T-shaped cross. This lack of any substantive Christian symbolism, though not unknown in religious buildings, when added to an absence of a structural chancel and the equivocal documentary descriptions (see below) has raised some doubt about the building's original use. The room was originally lit by three small east windows, now blocked, and two windows inserted into the earlier north wall which were later widened. The lack of windows on the more secure south side, the obvious place for good light, indicates that a building abutted here.

A great hall was established in the west range of the inner bailey, probably in the eleventh century. Its undercroft still exists with a broad central wall of plain arches – wide enough to have rubble facings between their dressed voussoirs, recalling similar work in the cathedral gallery. The undercroft is lit by small windows on its eastern courtyard side and, in its southern wall, a larger window was blocked when further rooms were added to this end of the hall. Along the southern side of the inner bailey, against the edge of the inner moat, the lowest levels of the present kitchen and garden stair building are of Norman date. Further to the east was an eleventh-century gatehouse leading out across the moat with a wall rising up to the motte again.

At the base of the motte on the east side of the courtyard was yet a further range of buildings, probably of late eleventh-century date, completely destroyed later in the medieval period. Recent excavations have shown this range to be of high status, with a herringbone-patterned floor as in the chapel and with painted wall plaster. At its northern end it almost abutted the chapel range and may have shared garderobe facilities with it as a finely arched drain exists in this corner of the courtyard.

Bishop Flambard is credited with the rebuilding of the gatehouse in the south range in the early twelfth century. Though much altered in later centuries, the surviving entrance arch with its thinly incised zigzag design looks similar to work in the cathedral nave. It has been suggested that Flambard may have also constructed the north range, remodelling rooms around the chapel, though the evidence for this is slight. Flambard is also known to have cleared Palace Green of buildings, linking the castle to the cathedral with walls and establishing the formal space between the two buildings, which he then lined with the offices of the palatinate. In this the bishop can be seen to be resolving the problem created when King William and Earl Waltheof located the castle in the best defensive position, at the northern end of the peninsula but away from the cathedral to the south. When the bishop acquired the earldom and the castle become his palace too, he would have found himself at the opposite end of the peninsula, away from his cathedral. The creation of Palace Green established a strong visual relationship and greatly facilitated the formalities of processing from bishop's palace to bishop's cathedral church.

By the middle of the twelfth century the castle at Durham covered an extensive area and the complexity of the inner bailey is well portrayed in an account written by Laurence, Prior of Durham *c.*1144-9:

> The area which this circuit of high walls surrounds is not empty or lacking in houses; it contains fine buildings. It displays two great palaces embellished with porticos, in which art itself is a sufficient recommendation of its artists. There is also a shining chapel here supported upon six columns not too large, but quite lovely. Here rooms adjoin rooms and buildings buildings, and each is devoted to its own special use. In this one the clothing is stored, in that one gleam the utensils, in this one there is a flash of armour . . . . On this side houses may thus be linked to houses and buildings to buildings, but on the other side as well there is no empty space. The centre of the castle however is free of buildings; instead that spot reveals a deep well of plentiful water.

Laurence's account raises several points of interest. Are the two 'palaces' the north and west ranges? Does the chapel 'supported *upon* six columns' refer to the surviving building or one, now gone, that may have stood above it? Perhaps most importantly, Laurence stresses, to the point of tedious repetition, the clutter of buildings. What survives is not the complete picture and many missing buildings need to be accounted for.

Around 1155 the west side of the town suffered a serious fire which badly damaged the castle. The rebuilding was undertaken by Bishop Hugh of Le Puiset (1153-95), a man whose episcopate, like that of the later John Cosin, represented a period of stability and reconstruction after years of turmoil and physical depredation in the city. He is said to have rebuilt the west range of the castle – the great hall – over the earlier undercroft, though physical evidence for this is hard to find. His major work was the rebuilding of the fire-damaged north range, where he erected double halls, one above the other, each probably with apartments at their east and west ends (**15**). A slight change in the wall alignment suggests earlier work may have been incorporated, though this is far from certain.

9 *Le Puiset's doorway in the castle's north range, as drawn by Billings in 1840.* Durham University Library

The lower hall was raised over an ancient sandbank, possibly a vestige of pre-Conquest or early Norman earthworks, and stood several feet above the courtyard level, supported by blank arcading and buttresses. Le Puiset gave this new hall a ceremonial entrance of such magnificence that it has no equal in the north of England (**9**). This entrance was originally external and approached by a flight of steps from the courtyard below. Like the best late Norman sculpture, it is lavishly and boldly cut, the arches covered in richly decorated designs of rosettes, zigzags and panel work (**colour plate 2**).

Almost all trace of Le Puiset's lower hall has disappeared internally in later alterations except for a short length of exposed zigzag string course and four windows, now concealed beneath the plasterwork in the University College Senior Common Room's south wall. The Norman gallery on the top storey of the north range represents the upper hall of Le Puiset's building. The whole of the south and most of the north walls survive as a continuous arcade of windows in alternate bays, their arches supported on columns, with raised bases forming window seats. The entire modulated composition is richly

10 *The Norman Gallery in the upper hall of Le Puiset's north range is a rare survival that illustrates the opulence of the twelfth-century castle.* Jarrold

decorated with zigzag (**10**), which must have graced one of the most magnificent suites of rooms in the Norman castle.

Le Puiset's range, though of the highest architectural quality, soon began to settle, particularly at the west end where the dramatic tilting can best be seen from below on Framwellgate Bridge. Early in the thirteenth century the north-west turret and garderobe tower were probably strengthened to buttress the building. Despite this, the castle at Durham at the end of the twelfth century had been transformed from its purely defensive function in 1072 into a castle-palace on a lavish scale, with few equals in the kingdom.

The later medieval castle 1284-1559

For over a century after the major additions to the castle by Le Puiset, successive thirteenth-century bishops saw no reason to enlarge or improve upon his work. It was not until the arrival of Bishop Bek (1284-1311) that once again major building began. He replaced the archaic and dimly-lit eleventh-century hall in the west range, constructing his great hall over its undercroft (**11**). Despite a great deal of later remodelling and alteration, the shell of much of the present building is Bek's. The finely arched entrance doorway is his and, almost opposite, the southernmost window on the west side of the hall retains its original jambs, head and inner arch, but with renewed tracery.

Bishop Hatfield (1345-81) made Bek's great hall even grander. He lengthened it southwards, renewed the roof and most of the windows on the east and west sides and inserted a double window, now partially blocked, in his new south wall (**colour plate 6**). At each end of the enlarged hall he placed a 'throne' and the surviving trumpeters' galleries on the east and west walls, though sometimes ascribed to both Bek and Fox, may be his too. They suggest Hatfield intended the hall to be a stage set to display episcopal power in ritual splendour and ceremony. The keep at this stage was a relic of the earliest Norman castle. Hatfield's decision to rebuild it required the motte to be widened, so blocking the east windows of the Norman chapel. The new keep was an irregular octagon, four storeys high over vaulted basements. Like the earlier shell keeps, apartments were lined against the outer walls leaving a central well open to the sky.

Why was it built? The old Norman keep would have been a very poor affair and the need for a 'last refuge' was important in a border castle like Durham.

11 *The castle courtyard from the keep. The west range incorporates Bek's great hall, first lengthened by Hatfield and later adapted by Fox (far left). Cosin's Black Stairs (centre) provide the link to the north range, with Tunstall's Gallery (right) standing before Le Puiset's remodelled double hall.* Jarrold

12 *A view of the peninsula from the west, painted in the early years of the eighteenth century. Hatfield's keep dominates the castle, surrounded by Cosin's terraced gardens above the town. Further south, in front of the cathedral another garden is visible, overlooked by a high observation tower or belvedere.* By kind permission of the Master of University College

The city had been attacked earlier in the century by the Scots and they again reached the outskirts of the town before their defeat at Neville's Cross in 1346. So defence was undoubtedly a major consideration. However, given Hatfield's sense of the bishopric's (or perhaps his own) importance, as expressed in his spectacular throne-tomb in the cathedral and the formality of his great hall, he would surely have relished the prospect of raising high above the town such a powerful symbol of his authority (**12**).

In the first half of the following century, the major developments were taking place just outside the main castle buildings, where Bishop Langley (1406-37) built the North Gate (see below) and Bishop Neville (1438-57) erected the exchequer at the outer gate of the barbican (**colour plate 13**). This is a rare survival, not dissimilar in function to the Jewel Tower at the Palace of Westminster, built to house the bishop's financial and legal records and accounts. It is the only one of the medieval bishops' administrative offices to remain. Its massive construction with small twin lancets is only relieved by Cosin's later traceried windows, which considerably lighten its façade. Hatfield's keep stood for over 100 years before the castle underwent a further major rebuilding programme during the episcopate of Bishop Fox (1494-1501). His work illustrates two important trends.

The first was the general decline in the military importance of castles, overtaken by improvements in artillery and new strategies of warfare. Such national trends, however, must be tempered by Durham's need to maintain a military role as a border castle long after contemporary buildings in southern England had lost that function. Nevertheless Langley's new North Gate at the beginning of the fifteenth century, while strengthening the peninsula, accelerated the redundancy of the castle's inner moat, a defensive earthwork so clogged up with refuse by this time that it had little practical value. The second development was the increasing emphasis placed on privacy and personal comfort in domestic architecture. Such benefits were usually lacking in the great military and religious buildings of the earlier medieval period where great halls, dormitories, refectories and infirmaries provided large uncomfortable spaces for communal living. The monasteries began to partition these open halls, and reserved their draughty refectories for special feast days only. This shift from communal living to private accommodation is discernible in military buildings too and Fox's work in Durham during his brief stay perfectly exemplifies the trend.

In the great hall in the west range, he reversed Hatfield's policy of enlargement, cutting off the southern end beyond the screens passage and creating four floors of apartments. He may well have done the same at the northern end too. Fox's reorganisation at the southern end of the hall led to the refurbishment of the service buildings, of which the kitchen is by far the most impressive room. Against the Norman south wall, two wide stone fireplaces were built and above them was raised a huge 'breastwork' in brick with angled relieving arches, central shaft and an embattled parapet – the earliest use of brick in Durham. In the kitchen's north wall he inserted a large arch for the buttery hatch. The buttery, scullery and brewhouse below were all built by 1499, as recorded on the timber-framed partition. Five hundred years later the smell of food still emanates from the kitchen and serving dishes still pass through its hatches (**13**).

Fox next planned to build a hall, kitchen and other rooms in Hatfield's keep but, before his plans were realised, he became Bishop of Winchester. Even the great improvements of Bishop Tunstall (1530-59) did not include finishing these new rooms in what must have seemed an increasingly inaccessible and redundant part of the castle. Tunstall's work represents quite the opposite: a gradual opening up of the medieval buildings. At the gatehouse he is said to have achieved a modest widening of the entrance passage by dismantling, raising and resetting the Norman archway and early Gothic vaulting. His main work was the construction of a new chapel linked to both the north and west ranges by a gallery with new staircase towers at the east and, probably, the west end too. This work, though unspectacular in its design, resolved a number of important functional and aesthetic problems in the north range. The gallery, in particular, was a response to the growing fashion for such rooms in the gentry

13 *The raised hatch of Bishop Fox's buttery, completed in 1499.* Royston Thomas

houses and palaces of the period. It also greatly eased the circulation problems caused by the subdivision of the range into smaller rooms and its buttressing of the lower walls must have helped stabilise Le Puiset's work. This Norman range, though impressive and innovative, was also gaunt and severe in its appearance from the courtyard. The gallery and chapel gave new modelling to its sheer south elevation. Tunstall's building, from the start, accommodated Bishop Ruthall's (1509-23) richly carved oak choir stalls, brought from Auckland Castle in 1547. This building was later lengthened by either Cosin or Crewe.

The gallery façade, lit by straight-headed, mullioned and transomed windows with round-headed lights, is emphasised by the larger window that lights Le Puiset's great doorway. The turret was even wider than earlier medieval spiral staircases and is designed with a fashionable Tudor half-octagon in the courtyard.

The decline of the castle-palace 1560–1659

The history of the castle has often been too easily explained by dividing it neatly into three periods relating to the building's use: border fortress 1072-1660, bishop's palace 1660-1832 and university college 1832 to the present day. At the beginning of this account the importance of the dual function of the Norman castle-palace has been stressed – there perhaps lies its greatest architectural importance.

The problem of its military decline must now be considered. It is a decline hard to document, especially during that somewhat 'dark age' period in Durham's architectural history from the Reformation to the Restoration (c.1540-1660). The castle moat in Owengate was clearly infilled and built upon in the fifteenth century, its gate gone by 1595. The evidence of the Fellows' Garden excavations in 1991 shows that, after a limited and ineffective recutting in the early fourteenth century, the castle moat at its western end was largely filled up too by the early sixteenth century, with Bishop Cosin's garden works representing the final infilling and levelling.

The Northgate barbican lost its military effectiveness in the middle of the fifteenth century and there is little evidence of any substantial military refortification of the peninsula walls after the Scottish threat in the first half of the fourteenth century. By 1574, the Dean and Chapter felt secure enough to erect a permanent new bridge across the Wear to their modest and unprotected Watergate postern. All this strongly suggests a substantial decline in military activity by the mid-sixteenth century at the latest.

In 1603, after the death of Elizabeth I, James VI of Scotland acceded to the English throne. Though formal union of the two countries was over a century away, and prejudice against the Scots continued long after that in the north-east of England, the accession signalled the final evaporation of Durham's military role as a border fortress. The castle-palace of the Norman bishops settled into the more sedate role of a comfortable episcopal residence. Little was done to the fabric of the castle in the first half of the seventeenth century. Bishop James installed the fine Jacobean fire surround now in the Senate Room and displayed the new king's coat of arms upon it, beside his own. Bishop Neile is said to have erected (or remodelled) the apartments within the north end of the great hall and formed the Senate suite at the east end of the north range.

During the Civil War and the Interregnum, with the bishopric abolished, the castle was sold in either 1649 or 1650 to Sir Thomas Andrews, draper and Lord Mayor of London. In 1650 it served as a prison hospital for 500 of the 3,000 Scottish prisoners brought from Dunbar after their defeat by Cromwell. In the years that followed, the building is said to have suffered greatly from damage and neglect, compounded by the long period of building inactivity. At the Restoration, the castle is recorded as belonging to Susan Blakiston, widow of John Blakiston, judge at the trial of Charles I and brother-in-law of John Cosin. Whether she occupied it as owner or tenant is unclear but the prospect of Bishop John Cosin returning to dispossess his sister-in-law reinforces the commonly held view that Durham was then, as now, 'a small world'.

14 *The Black Stairs of 1662 were the most spectacular and influential of Bishop Cosin's many improvements to the medieval castle.* Durham University Library: Edis Collection Ca26

The bishop's palace 1660-1832

At the Restoration in 1660, when Bishop John Cosin (1660-72) returned triumphantly to the city, he immediately began work on both his cathedral church and his castle. Much of this is recorded in his private correspondence and many of the building contracts survive. The castle in Durham was at first unfit for Cosin to stay in and, in early 1662, on his occasional visits from London, he was still in lodgings. The inadequacies of the medieval castle quickly became apparent and, to resolve the cramped circulation between the two main ranges, he gave priority to the construction of a new staircase, the Black Stairs. Cosin required the design of the stair tower to reflect Tunstall's turret:

> for if the outward stone case be not made to answer the Towre at the other end of the gallery leading up to the chappell, I shall not like the cost of a new stayre.
>
> *(February 1662)*

Its architecture was certainly respectful and conservative but inside such reticence was abandoned. The magnificent staircase is one of the finest of its time in England, rising through four floors built around a large open well (**14**). Made of painted pine, its balustrades have richly carved baroque foliage designs with a high moulded handrail, an old-fashioned but practical detail, being easy to grip.

The stair tower was lit from above by a lantern with an ogee-shaped cap, matching one on Tunstall's turret which was heightened about the same time. A third lantern graced the gateway, creating collectively a far more interesting roofline around the courtyard than at present (**15**). Sadly all have now gone. The cantilevered stairs eventually settled, leaned inwards and required the insertion of what have generously been called Tuscan columns between the newel posts. Pit props would have been nearer the mark.

The great hall remained Cosin's ceremonial building and he did a considerable amount of work on it. He panelled the walls, remodelled Neile's north end chamber and, at the southern end, erected a 'screen of wainscot' bearing, as so often on his buildings, his coat of arms. Outside, Cosin remodelled the main entrance façade, contracting James Oliphant, John Richardson and Christopher Wilkinson in 1663-4 to construct the classical porch and encase the medieval buttresses in new stonework, finished with little ogee tops, similar to his chapel at Auckland, and recalling his earlier chapel at Pembroke College, Cambridge. Cosin's joiners and carpenters were much employed throughout the building, though attributions are scarce. John and Anthony Smith are recorded working in the library and on the chapel organ in 1665, and the bishop's Dutch painter, Jan Baptist Van Eersell, temporarily resident in Claypath, was contracted in 1664 to paint, gild and varnish the screens in the gallery. He also painted the

15 *The castle from the south, in the early eighteenth century, showing Cosin's and Crewe's improvements. The Norman exterior of Le Puiset's north range is more evident, before its eighteenth-century re-façading. Cosin's terraced motte (right) and moat gardens (foreground) are well-illustrated.* By kind permission of the Master of University College

'great stares', presumably with the dark staining used on much of Cosin's woodwork, which masked their softwood origins and thus rendered them 'Black'. The same prefix had been given to Cosin's audience chamber in the Great Hall. From here either Cosin himself or his successor, Crewe, would have invited honoured guests to step out of the gloomy dark interior, through the castle wall, onto a brightly-painted balcony perched precariously out over the banks. Here, still squinting in the sun, they would experience the expansive change of space and the panorama of the town and river.

In the castle's north range, in about 1670, Hatfield's roof was replaced and repairs were also carried out in Tunstall's chapel including the provision of new screens. Whether it was Cosin or Crewe who extended the chapel eastwards is debatable but, in doing so, they reused Tunstall's original east window in the new work. Cosin's work on the principal ranges of his restored palace was complemented by improvements to the barbican, courtyard and gardens (chapter 6). During his energetic tenure he had transformed the neglected fabric of the medieval palace, giving it a grandeur and richness that most benefited his successor Nathaniel Crewe who spent much of his long episcopate (1674-1722) in Durham rather than at Auckland Castle (**12**). He entertained on a lavish scale and his new apartments in the Norman Gallery, the enlarged chapel and the extra doors in the lower gallery, all in the north range, may have been a response to the numerous guests who would have stayed here. Likewise, his repair of the ruinous keep in 1714 may have been to spare his own blushes by avoiding the risk of falling masonry.

Commodious as the apartments at Durham undoubtedly were, they lay within a cramped medieval site, accessible through an equally cramped and insanitary medieval city. Auckland Castle by comparison was less constrained, healthier and set within expansive gardens and parkland. Little wonder the eighteenth-century bishops increasingly preferred it to Durham. Bishop Butler (1750-2) had little chance to enjoy either, dying shortly after his arrival. He did, however, instigate repairs and improvements in the north range, continued by his successor Bishop Trevor (1752-71). Le Puiset's range had always caused structural problems and, between 1751 and 1756, extensive repairs were carried out under the direction of Sanderson Miller, a well-known designer in the Gothic style.

The north wall was largely rebuilt, and the leaning south wall cut back and straightened by a new face of stonework, supported on beams in the Tunstall gallery roof. Although this undoubtedly saved the building, it destroyed the surface modelling on Le Puiset's south elevation created by the shallow buttresses and the twin light openings still visible at the top of the Black Stairs (**15**). Much flatter traceried sash windows with ogee heads in characteristic Gothic Revival manner were substituted.

Miller's main employment in the range was the remodelling and decoration of the bishop's dining room, now the Senior Common Room (**16**). He inserted two big Gothic traceried sash windows with delicate matching panelling in the deep embrasures of the Norman walls. Each window was topped by ogee mouldings and between them he placed the large stone fireplace in the same style. The fifteenth-century ceiling was relatively undisturbed save for a gilded cornice of trefoils and the strange ornament beneath the moulded beams, likened by one member of the Senior Common Room to strawberry tarts!

Bishop Egerton (1771-87) continued the refurbishment in this range. He formed the Octagon and refitted the Senate Room with its mid-seventeenth century Flemish tapestries. The eighteenth-century bishops had all concentrated their building activities on the north range, where their comfortable private apartments and generous reception rooms made life tolerably civilised within the walls of a Norman castle. The great hall by comparison offered little scope for adaptation and Hatfield's keep was even more of a medieval anachronism. Isolated and uninhabited for over 250 years, it was ruined and dangerous, and in 1789, Bishop Thurlow demolished the upper storeys to make the building safe (**36**).

16 *The gatehouse, Norman in origin, has been much altered over the centuries. It was extensively remodelled and enlarged in the late eighteenth century to the designs of James Wyatt.* Royston Thomas

The final embellishment to the episcopal castle was made by Bishop Barrington in 1791, when James Wyatt remodelled the gatehouse. The core of the medieval building was retained, supplemented by a heightened central tower and flanking lodges, decorated with the familiar hallmarks of eighteenth-century Gothic – the crosslet and quatrefoil. The whole building was finished with battlements that were also carried the length of Cosin's barbican walls to the outer gate piers. This was the last major building in the castle by the bishops of Durham. In 1832 the new University of Durham was founded and, by 1840, Auckland Castle became the sole episcopal home, though the bishop retained a small suite of rooms for his use should business detain him in Durham overnight.

University College 1832-2002

The university had originally been promised the castle, but Bishop Van Mildert's reluctance to move led in 1834 to Anthony Salvin's design for an ambitious new college in the south-west corner of Palace Green. The scheme was abandoned when Bishop Maltby finally vacated the castle and work concentrated on the adaptation of the ruined keep for student rooms. Salvin was retained and undertook its rebuilding in 1839-40, keeping the irregular octagonal plan and possibly incorporating some material from the old keep in his new work (**colour plate 5**).

In 1847 the great hall's north window was restored and, in 1882, to commemorate the fiftieth anniversary of the university, it was reglazed in stained glass by Kempe. At the same time the hall received its oak panelling and screen, replacing Cosin's original work. The work in the castle this century has concentrated on conservation of the fabric and the sensitive adaptations and adjustments necessary to keep a Norman episcopal castle functioning as a modern university college. Major structural repairs were carried out on the west side of the castle in the 1930s and in 1952 the Norman chapel was restored.

A co-ordinated conservation programme was begun in 1987 with the cleaning of Le Puiset's doorway in the north range, followed by repairs to the gatehouse and north range (north wall). Not that all work is repair. New administrative offices in a minimalist Tudor style by castle architect, Dennis Jones, were built in the Fellows' Garden in 1993.

The river moat

In a book about buildings and manmade landscapes, it is easy to ignore the obvious natural characteristics of the Durham peninsula that led to its successful occupation for over a thousand years. Before examining the medieval development of the castle and town walls, the role of the river needs emphasising and we need to assess the military impact of some of the modifications made to it. The castle at Durham was not just the motte and inner bailey, it was the whole peninsula, and the river was its natural moat. Only the northern neck of land required substantial fortification. That impassable moat was always effective, provided that the river ran deep and strong, and that it was not bridged or otherwise obstructed.

The early Norman city was accessible only by fords on its western and eastern sides. Bishop Flambard's Framwellgate Bridge of *c*.1120 provided easy access for all, from traders in the town to pilgrims to the cathedral. Conversely, of course, it would also aid those who might attack the town and so it needed fortification with gate towers. Was Flambard's bridge a single isolated event or was it part of a broader infrastructure improvement that also had significant military benefits?

The increased population of both the peninsula citadel and the surrounding town would have needed a steady supply of flour for bread. To meet this demand, water-powered mills with weirs were provided. The weirs not only provided steady power to the mills but also ensured a constant supply of deep water in the river, essential for military security. But these benefits would result in the flooding of the old fords, hence the need to build a bridge.

There is clearly an inter-relationship between river moat, ford, mill, weir and bridge that needs examining. It is far from clear whether these urban developments were separate or conceived as a co-ordinated project. In all this we should not ignore the role of Ranulf Flambard, a builder-bishop whose work in twelfth-century Durham demonstrates a holistic view of what we would call todayΔ town planning. Without firmer evidence little more can be said, but it was the constant and impassable flow of water around the peninsula that was the essential prerequisite for the defence of the citadel.

Castle and town walls

The earliest peninsula defences, possibly of Anglo-Saxon date, were rebuilt by Bishop Flambard. From the motte the wall ran east to the North Gate, the principal entrance onto the peninsula, then south around the river gorge, along the edge of the higher ground, with gates to the east (Kingsgate) and south (Watergate) (17). Flambard also built a wall between the keep and the cathedral, having cleared Palace Green of houses to establish his administrative centre and reinforce the relationship between his castle-palace and his cathedral. Le Puiset rebuilt, and presumably strengthened, the walls along the east side of the peninsula in 1173-4, defences possibly damaged in the earlier Cumin usurpation. Later still a wall was constructed from the east end of the cathedral down Bow Lane to Kingsgate to divide the civil and ecclesiastical precincts. The gateway in this wall, across North Bailey, was later incorporated into the church tower of St Mary-le-Bow.

The Scottish incursions into northern England in the early years of the fourteenth century led to the strengthening of the castle in Durham; the bastion tower, situated between the keep and the North Gate, most probably dates from this period. Certainly the North Gate would have been kept in good repair and in 1313, after Robert Bruce's raid into the suburbs of Durham, a number of properties were removed from the front of the gate for a barbican to be built. It should be stressed that the reinforcement of the city's defences in the early fourteenth century was concentrated solely on the heavily fortified north wall, already reinforced by the castle keep and the North Gate – a formidable line. Nothing was done around the rest of the peninsula, a clear indication that the river served very effectively as a castle moat – deep and difficult to cross.

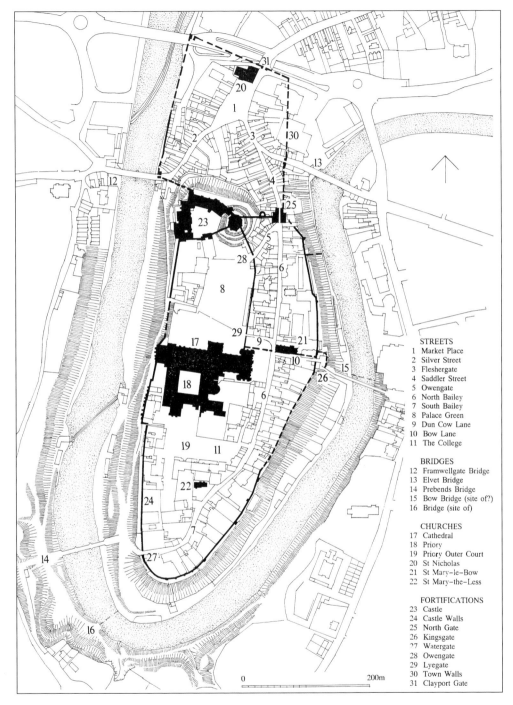

STREETS
1 Market Place
2 Silver Street
3 Fleshergate
4 Saddler Street
5 Owengate
6 North Bailey
7 South Bailey
8 Palace Green
9 Dun Cow Lane
10 Bow Lane
11 The College

BRIDGES
12 Framwellgate Bridge
13 Elvet Bridge
14 Prebends Bridge
15 Bow Bridge (site of?)
16 Bridge (site of)

CHURCHES
17 Cathedral
18 Priory
19 Priory Outer Court
20 St Nicholas
21 St Mary-le-Bow
22 St Mary-the-Less

FORTIFICATIONS
23 Castle
24 Castle Walls
25 North Gate
26 Kingsgate
27 Watergate
28 Owengate
29 Lyegate
30 Town Walls
31 Clayport Gate

17 *The Norman peninsula defences lay south of the castle, along the edge of the river gorge, protecting the cathedral, the priory and the palatinate's administrative buildings on Palace Green. To the north lay the early fourteenth-century rectangular enclosure of the town walls around the Market Place*

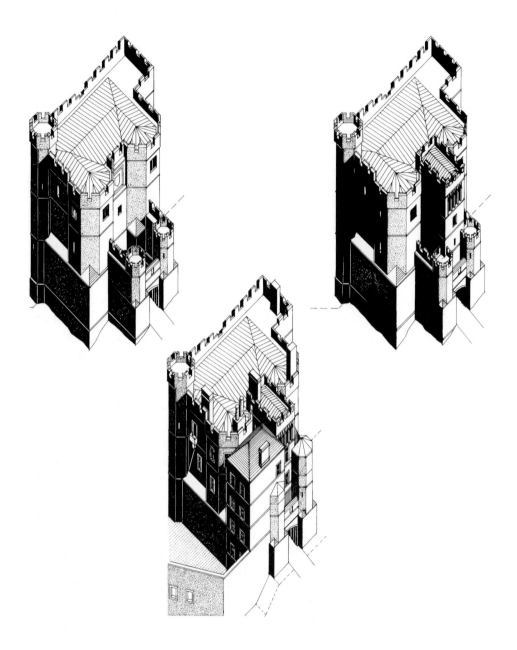

18 *The North Gate as it may have looked (above left) on completion around 1421, (above right) after the late fifteenth-century addition of a central wing over the barbican, and (below) following improvements of 1790 including a new wing and exercise yard. The abutment of the castle wall is not shown*

The refortification of the peninsula citadel was all very well but it did little to protect the town from Bruce's almost annual visits. So, in 1315 the towns-people successfully petitioned the King for permission to protect the Bishop's Borough around the Market Place with walls. New gates were constructed at Walkergate, Clayport and on Elvet Bridge, while that already on Framwellgate Bridge was probably strengthened. Early the next century the old North Gate was rebuilt by Bishop Langley (completed 1421). It incorporated a new gaol, replacing an earlier prison that had been built on the west side of Palace Green where the Exchequer now stands. This new gate was a very imposing structure indeed and was as much an expression of episcopal power as a necessary piece of military architecture (**18**). The main gateway was flanked by large polygonal towers, with the gaol rising above it. In front was an open barbican with smaller turrets beside the outer gate and portcullis. Later in the fifteenth century the barbican's defensive function was eliminated when it was covered by a tall wing set forward of the main towers. The new wing faced to the north with a showy display of shields, ornately canopied windows and battlements more like the belfry of a church tower (**36**).

The military importance of the castle's peninsula walls declined during the sixteenth century and the gates on Elvet Bridge and at the top of Owengate had gone by 1595. The gradual opening-up of the city in the seventeenth and eighteenth centuries is chronicled elsewhere (chapter 5), but throughout the period the North Gate remained.

By the end of the eighteenth century, the poor and very public accommo-dation of the prisoners in the gaol was causing concern. John Howard's unfavourable reports of 1777 and 1784 led to only slight improvements in 1790. By the early years of the nineteenth century, a new gaol was under construction and in 1820, following the transfer of prisoners, the old North Gate was taken down, the last medieval gate of Durham to be removed. Although the gates disappeared during the post-medieval period, the peninsula walls remained. They were not free-standing walls that could easily be taken down, but retained higher ground on the Baileys. On the west side they were also enmeshed in the monastic and late prebendal buildings of the cathedral.

What then is left of the peninsula fortifications? Along its northern line lies the best feature, the large early fourteenth-century bastion tower, which stood complete until collapses in 1774 and 1820. It is semi-circular in plan and was originally at least four storeys high. In the early eighteenth century, the tower's circular roof top was laid out as a small formal garden, its brick parapet embell-ished with stone decorations. The ground and first floors of this tower survive, each half octagonal room having five arched recesses with arrow loops enabling full protection to be given to the adjoining castle wall.

The remains of the North Gate are fragmentary, dispersed but extraordi-narily tantalising. They demonstrate, that like so much in Durham, when old documents talk of demolition, it was rarely comprehensive and much survived to be incorporated into the new building. If this is true of the 1820 demolition, it is also true of the North Gate's early fifteenth-century rebuilding, which evidently included earlier, possibly Norman, fabric.

In the basement of 46 Saddler Street, appropriately used until recently as the University's Archaeology Department, students refreshed themselves in a kitchen hard against the exposed ashlar plinth of the barbican's north-east turret. Across the road at 2 Owengate, the back wall of this 1820s brick house reveals ancient masonry to a great height and, in the adjacent Owengate House, deep below the road level, accessible along a narrow passage is a perfect little stone vaulted chamber of the crispest fifteenth century ashlar. Many other examples survive, dislocated parts awaiting survey and analysis.

From the North Gate the wall runs south-east to the edge of the plateau, arches over a sand gully where foundations were impossible to construct, and on to an angle turret whose fine ashlar resembles Le Puiset's work. It was well placed to protect his new Elvet Bridge over the river below. Southwards, a spur wall is said to have led off down to the river, ending in a tower. Certainly such spurs are essential if the river's moat function was to be maintained. At Hatfield College, engravings of the late seventeenth century show a large square tower, whose lower walls are supposed to be embedded in the present buildings. Kingsgate, at the bottom of Bow Lane, has gone but some remains of its small barbican may be buried within the terrace wall overlooking Kingsgate Bridge. This wall, with its decorative stone and brickwork, is the last surviving length of the once extensive seventeenth-century embroidery of the medieval castle walls.

Between Kingsgate and Watergate the wall line is generally known but the dating is more imprecise. The stretch behind St John's College is coursed rubble and, though the embattled towers in their garden setting look eighteenth century, in their lower courses the masonry plinths look medieval. On the extreme southern end of the peninsula is one of the best stretches of the wall, closely buttressed, possibly to support small turrets to oversee the tightly curving defences (**71**). In the south-west corner, the present Watergate of late eighteenth-century date replaced a single arched postern. It is designed with a plain semi-circular arched opening as a fitting prelude to the classical architecture of Prebends Bridge (George Nicholson 1772-8).

On the west side along Prebends Walk the wall is domestic in character and clearly post-medieval in date but, as it approaches the cathedral, it becomes increasingly absorbed into the fabric of the former priory buildings. At Dark Entry the alignment suddenly changes, then resumes its course further west. This protruding angle may have given protection to the postern gate but may also mark a deliberate shift in the line of the walls by Flambard, or one of the later Norman bishops, anticipating the clutter of buildings that would crowd into this corner of the monastery. This was certainly the case, and the walls between Dark

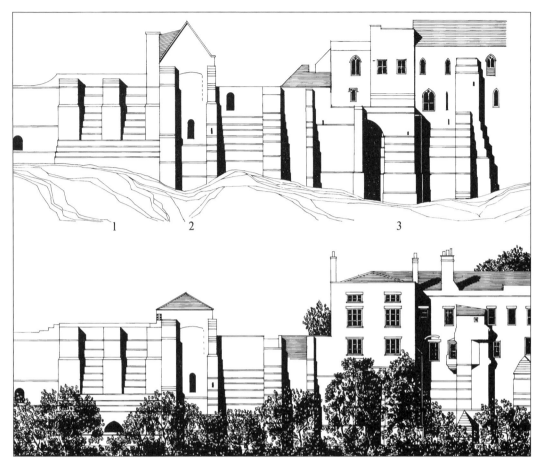

19 *The peninsula walls to the west of the priory supported many of the monastic buildings. Their appearance in the late eighteenth century (above) reveals the extent of the medieval fabric which had survived until then, and which is still incorporated within the present buildings (below). From the left are the lower levels of the reredorter (1), the so-called 'prison' below the Master of the Infirmary's lodgings (2) and the infirmary (3)*

Entry and the Galilee, supporting the medieval guest hall, infirmary, infirmary's lodgings and reredorter, are the most impressive and instructive on the peninsula (**19**). The original wall was buttressed and can be identified by its many chamfered offsets. It has required further support from still larger buttresses that both restrain the outward thrust of the walls and support the monastic buildings that project above the river banks. Latrine outfalls are much in evidence, none greater than the large drain from the mid-twelfth-century reredorter.

From here to the Galilee the wall contains a mural passage. This may have originally extended along the boundary of the monastic precincts and enabled access for the garrison along the walls without disturbing the privacy of the priory. The passage was made redundant when the Galilee severed its link to the castle. The Galilee itself was probably built off the original castle wall and to the north the wall cuts back, pierced only by the postern at Windy Gap, before rejoining the castle across the inner moat.

North of the castle the early fourteenth-century town walls have almost completely vanished. However, portions remain in the lower parts of the riverside buildings on the west side, and lengths of rubble masonry on the east behind Elvet Bridge may be small remnants. The wall was never as substantial as the castle wall and, to judge by the engravings of Clayport, its gates were barely fortified with only vehicular and pedestrian arches. There were no flanking towers nor any manifestations of civic pride and wellbeing.

3
THE CATHEDRAL

The Anglo-Saxon churches

When the Community of St Cuthbert arrived on the peninsula at Durham in 995, they erected 'a little church of boughs of trees' as a shelter for the body of their saint. Soon afterwards, a more substantial church was erected – the *Alba Ecclesia*, the 'White Church' – presumably constructed of limewashed wattle and daub. It remained in use for three years while Bishop Aldhun's *Ecclesia Major* was built in stone. This church was consecrated on 4 September 998 and survived until the construction of the great Romanesque cathedral. No structural remains of it have yet been found, but a late twelfth-century description tells of two stone towers with bronze pinnacles, one at the west end and one over the choir, suggesting a cruciform church with a crossing tower. The west tower, unfinished by Aldhun, was completed by his successor, Eadmund, between 1021 and 1042.

Where did the church stand? The evidence of documentary sources strongly suggests it lay south of the present cathedral, broadly within the confines of the existing cloister. In medieval times there stood in the cloister garth, opposite the slype door, a tomb with a statue of St Cuthbert. This has been interpreted as a cenotaph, marking the place where the saint's body lay in the Anglo-Saxon church, at the east end behind the high altar. Recent geophysical examination of the cloister garth has failed for the second time to find any evidence for this church. This is not of course conclusive proof that it did not stand there, only that its walls and foundations may have been very comprehensively removed. This failure does, however, throw into greater prominence alternative views on the early churches. So, into this orderly sequential development of one church replacing another, there is the possibility that the Community had more than one church in use at the same time: that they retained the earlier church beside the new one. This was not an uncommon feature of Anglo-Saxon monasteries; there are parallels at Jarrow and Hexham. Some scholars suggest this also happened at Durham. If two such churches did exist, it would conveniently explain the destruction of one church, documented as taking place at the time of the laying of the foundations of the Norman church in 1093, allowing the shrine of St Cuthbert to be protected by the other until the translation of the body in 1104.

The coming of the Normans

In 1071 Walcher was appointed as the first Norman bishop. He planned to regularise the secular Community of St Cuthbert and, in anticipation of this, began to construct new monastic buildings, commencing with the east range. Following Walcher's murder in 1080, his successor, William of St Calais, installed Benedictine monks in 1083. He intended to advance the works on the monastic buildings, a layout that anticipated the building of a new church north of the cloisters. However, in 1088 his treason against the King led to his exile for three years. Meanwhile the monks continued with the rebuilding.

St Calais spent his exile in Normandy. Whatever his plans were beforehand to continue Walcher's work, his time spent in France effected a radical change in his thinking. In 1092, a year after his return, he proposed the rebuilding of the Anglo-Saxon cathedral, not of the modest size matching Walcher's cloister, but on an altogether larger scale.

The Romanesque cathedral

> Durham Cathedral was hardly surpassed in its day, and has about it the air of serene finality which belongs of right to the greatest masterpieces. It represents the summit of achievement.
>
> *(K. Conant)*

The construction of the great cathedral church, by Bishops St Calais and Flambard between 1093 and 1133, is the central architectural event in the history of Durham. What circumstances led to the construction of such a masterpiece in Durham at that time? Why is it so historically important and what creates its aesthetic perfection?

Romanesque architecture was a European style distinguished by several varying regional 'schools', of which the Norman school was a significant example. The first appearance of the style in England was King Edward the Confessor's church at Westminster Abbey (begun *c*.1050). With the Norman invasion in 1066 there began a prodigious campaign of building activity in the late eleventh and early twelfth centuries. There was scarcely a single cathedral, abbey or parish church that was not rebuilt in the new style.

The new Anglo-Norman churches were distinguished by their great size, such as those at Canterbury (begun *c*.1070), Lincoln (begun *c*.1072) and Winchester (begun 1079) – one of the largest in Europe. A great many of these are now lost and so the process by which the Romanesque style developed in England, and particularly its route to Durham, is difficult to follow. Most of these early churches were planned from the start with flat wooden ceilings over

20 *The vaulting of the nave, looking east, fully demonstrates both the sense of spatial unity and the dynamic tension that the use of ribs can achieve.* Royston Thomas

their choir and nave – the vaulting of wide spans in stone was still a great problem for Romanesque masons in the late eleventh century. It was, however, desirable for aesthetic and practical reasons, and experiments had been undertaken in churches in continental Europe.

In 1091 St Calais returned from exile to Durham, the border town and resting place of the greatest of the northern saints, with its troubled history of insurrection and rebellion. The need to construct a powerful and, above all, fireproof symbol of Norman dominance would have been impressed upon him. He obtained the services of an unknown master mason of exceptional genius, familiar with the work on the great new English churches and aware of structural advances in Europe.

Durham was the first major English church to be covered entirely with a stone vault and one of the earliest buildings in Europe to use ribbed vaulting throughout, an advance that offered profound aesthetic improvements (**20**). The master masons of Romanesque Europe were striving to achieve an architectural unity inside their churches. Spanning the walls of a church with a flat wooden ceiling only reinforced the separateness of each element: wall-roof-wall. Barrel and groin vaulting represented a major aesthetic advance as the elements are integrated, the vault springing naturally from the wall tops.

Groin vaults funnelled the thrust to the corners of the bay enabling larger clerestory windows. Though early rib vaults may have had little structural advantages over the groin vault, visually they were a great advance, the eye focusing on the ribs, the slender lines of thrust that spanned across the vault. Diagonal ribs, in a building of rectilinear elements, added yet another dimension, and a highly dynamic one, to the composition. Vaulting over square bays with only semi-circular ribs causes aesthetic and structural difficulties – the diagonals needing to be higher than the enclosing ribs. In the choir at Durham this problem was avoided by dividing the square bay into two oblong bays, so reducing the height of the diagonal ribs. The crown of the vault remained broadly level throughout. Later, in the nave, pointed transverse ribs improved the overall directional aspect of the interior by completely levelling the crown of the vault.

That directional movement was subtly modified by the double bay system of the nave and choir arcades. Instead of identical piers that draw the eye quickly to the east end, the alternate primary and secondary piers slow the eye's progress and create a more complex and modulated rhythm down the body of the church. Durham represented the culmination of the structural and aesthetic advances of European Romanesque architecture. The sense of spatial unity was without comparison. Once achieved at Durham, the foundations had been laid for the gradual emergence of the Gothic style during the course of the twelfth century.

Development of the Norman church

On 11 August 1093 the foundation stones for the new church were laid, amid great ceremony (**21**). The funds accumulated for the work must have been vast as the work proceeded with great speed. St Calais died in 1096 and the monks continued the work with some hesitancy until Bishop Flambard's arrival three years later. He found the church 'made as far as the nave' and, during his episcopate, the work progressed more slowly, with the translation of St Cuthbert's body into the newly vaulted sanctuary in 1104.

The documentary evidence tells of the demolition of the Anglo-Saxon church when the foundations of the new church were laid in 1093. This poses the question of what happened to St Cuthbert's shrine between 1093 and translation in 1104? Either the shrine portion of the old Anglo-Saxon church would have stood substantially intact until this ceremony or, for advocates of the double church theory, one church was demolished and one remained to hold the body of the saint. After the translation of St Cuthbert, work continued westward and at Flambard's death in 1128 the nave walls had been constructed; the nave vault was added by 1133, thus completing the church except for the upper stages of the towers.

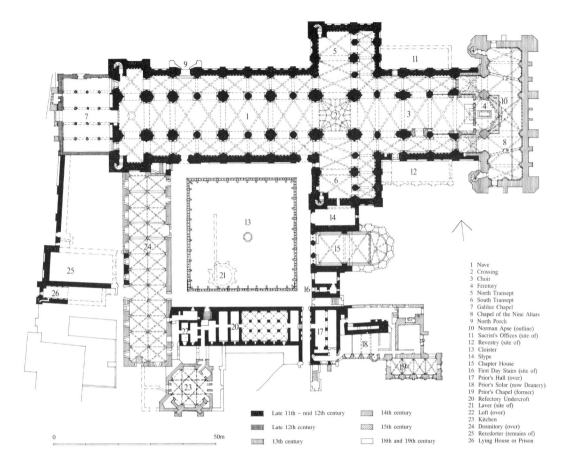

1 Nave
2 Crossing
3 Choir
4 Feretory
5 North Transept
6 South Transept
7 Galilee Chapel
8 Chapel of the Nine Altars
9 North Porch
10 Norman Apse (outline)
11 Sacrist's Offices (site of)
12 Revestry (site of)
13 Cloister
14 Slype
15 Chapter House
16 First Day Stairs (site of)
17 Prior's Hall (over)
18 Prior's Solar (now Deanery)
19 Prior's Chapel (former)
20 Refectory Undercroft
21 Laver (site of)
22 Loft (over)
23 Kitchen
24 Dormitory (over)
25 Reredorter (remains of)
26 Lying House or Prison

Late 11th – mid 12th century   14th century

Late 12th century   15th century

13th century   18th and 19th century

0   50m

21 *The plan of the cathedral and the claustral buildings*

The plan of the church was cruciform and based upon the double bay arcade design. The building was aisled throughout except for the west side of the transepts. Two double bays formed the choir, then a crossing and three more, plus two oblong bays, formed the nave. The transepts each had two double bays, one with a single vault. The east end was terminated by an apse around the shrine of St Cuthbert, with aisles ending in chapels, apsidal within but square externally, a plan form originating in the Romanesque abbey churches in Normandy and adopted in England at St Albans and Lincoln, for example. The transeptal chapels were square throughout and the nave was completed with a pair of western towers. There was a north porch at the west end of the nave and both transepts had stair turrets.

The vertical subdivision of the church was comprised of the arcade with alternating compound piers and cylindrical columns, above a gallery with twin openings under a single containing arch for each bay of the arcade, and a narrow clerestory within the lunettes of the vaulting. The Romanesque cathedral church was the design of a mason-architect of genius. A consummate engineer with the most subtle aesthetic sensibilities, his work nevertheless underwent a number of significant changes in the course of its construction. The building of the church began at the east end, the only part of the original plan to have been lost.

The eastern apse, choir and crossing

St Calais' east end, surrounding the high altar (sanctuary) and St Cuthbert's Shrine (feretory), was destroyed by the construction of the Chapel of the Nine Altars in the thirteenth century. From the remains of the apse, still surviving beneath the feretory floor, and the evidence of variations in the easternmost portions of the choir, it is possible to suggest the original form. Internally the great apse supported a semi-domed vault, whilst externally with the adjoining bay it was probably roofed at a slightly lower level than the main choir. The remains of spiral staircases over the choir aisle apses indicate that turrets at least were intended here, possibly even taller towers, as in the Rhineland churches.

The choir and crossing form the earliest surviving part of the Romanesque church. The proportions of the arcade and gallery within the double bay system are followed throughout the whole building. Earlier single bay designs in England had either balanced the proportions of the arcade, triforium gallery and clerestory (Norwich and Peterborough) or over-emphasised the arcade at the expense of the triforium (Gloucester and Tewkesbury). At Durham the relationship is more considered and dynamic, and the counterpoint created between the elements within the double bay is far more subtle. The cylindrical piers throughout the church are boldly incised, with spiral decoration in the eastern parts, with lozenges, zigzags and fluting in the nave. The designs were prefabricated as the adjustments at the joints clearly show. Though they may have more than decorative significance, the visual impact of the designs, in disguising the bulkiness of the piers, is stunning and innovative on such a scale (**colour plate 7**).

The choir and its aisles were designed to receive rib vaults and, in the choir aisles, every vault rib has its corresponding shaft rising from the floor. This results in the unsatisfactory imposition of shafts on the aisle side of the circular columns, a practice abandoned in the nave. Within the choir itself, triple attached shafts at the gallery level were prepared to receive the high vault. This vault was replaced in the thirteenth century, but its line can still be seen against the wall of the choir clerestory. Within the gallery of the choir there are semi-circular transverse arches to every bay; later in the nave there were quarter or quadrant arches in the same position. These have been interpreted as early examples of flying buttresses, counteracting the lateral thrust of the high vault. In fact, as originally constructed, they only lightly abutted the main walls and were probably intended as support for the gallery roof timbers.

22 *Several of the gallery windows on the north side of the cathedral still retain evidence (to the right of the window) of the original Norman gablets.* Royston Thomas

The original arrangement of these gallery roofs was very different from their present appearance. In the nave they had lower abutments to the wall and individual gablets to every bay, still evident on the north side – an arrangement difficult to conjecture (**22**). It was, however, sufficiently awkward to have necessitated the present simpler solution during the thirteenth century.

The transepts

The construction of the transepts probably coincided with the death of St Calais in 1096 and the accession of Flambard in 1099. It marks the first period of hesitation in the building programme, almost certainly brought on by a lack of finance. The cost of construction during the vacancy was borne entirely by the monks who could not match the bishops' munificence. Even after Flambard's arrival, work fluctuated and changes in the roofing of the church are evident.

In the south transept, where work was more advanced than in the north, the idea of a high vault was abandoned around 1104, and the clerestory was built in anticipation of a timber ceiling. The ceiling was probably constructed and a similar ceiling presumably planned for the north transept until an influx of funds enabled the upper parts of this transept to be designed for, and to receive, a rib vault, around 1110. When the south transept was finally vaulted, (c.1110–1120) with fashionable zigzag ornament, it blocked the openings of the original clerestory.

The nave

Bishop Flambard found the church in 1099 built 'as far as the nave'. This may mean little more than the foundations of the western walls and piers. It seems likely that the main work up to 1104 concentrated on completing the choir vault and continuing with the crossing and transepts to the west. It was also necessary to build the first two eastern bays of the nave arcade, with their adjoining aisle vaults, and a single bay of the gallery above to buttress the choir vault and high crossing. The nave may well have been intended to be roofed in wood at this stage but, when work continued after around 1110, Flambard's use of zigzag on ribs and arches clearly identifies the second building campaign when the high vaulting was continued (**23**). The absence of zigzag on the interlacing arches of the aisle walls has led some commentators to speculate that the entire enclosure of the church may have been completed at low level before around 1110.

In the building of the nave, two improvements were made, one established during the first campaign, the second a much later introduction. The problem of the choir aisle shafts abutting the cylindrical columns was overcome by omitting them altogether in the nave, and enlarging the diameter of the column to absorb the vaulting ribs. The second modification was the use of pointed transverse arches across the nave's high vault at some time between 1128 and 1133. This was a significant use of the pointed arch for structural and aesthetic purposes.

The nave was entered through four great portals that exhibit fine figurative, as well as decorative, sculpture in their capitals and arches. The Prior's Door in the cloisters is a particularly fine late twelfth-century example by Bishop Hugh of Le Puiset, but noticeably less grand than that he installed at the entrance to his new hall in the castle. Affixed to the door of the north portal is the celebrated bronze sanctuary knocker (replica on door, original in the treasury) of around 1180, symbol of the protection given by the priory to fugitives who were able to reach the security of the church and churchyard. Over the medieval north porch there were originally said to be two chambers where monks maintained a constant vigil to admit those who sought sanctuary. Recent research has confirmed the existence of the rooms but doubts their function. It is thought they may have served some liturgical purpose related to the porch's importance as the principal entrance for processions and ceremonies.

The west front

The west end of the cathedral was designed as an impressive façade, flanked by twin towers, perched high above the river gorge. It was largely complete at the time of Flambard's death in 1128. Le Puiset may have completed the building of the narrow heavily zigzagged gable lights before starting on the Galilee but work on the upper stages of the western towers was not recommenced until around 1195-1208, in an early Gothic style, and probably continued into the

23 *The eastern bays of the nave indicate the break in the construction during the early years of the twelfth century. The later work, beginning around 1110, is characterised by the use of zigzag ornament on the arches of the nave arcade and gallery (upper centre) compared to the earlier work (upper left).* Royston Thomas

early decades of the century. Though the original arrangement of the west front has been altered by the Galilee and great west window, there remains sufficient evidence for Ian Curry to suggest a possible reconstruction (**24**).

Patron and master mason: influences and sources

The story of building the original design of the great Norman cathedral at Durham effectively ends with the completion of the west front and the temporary abandonment of raising its western towers. Before describing the later additions and changes to the fabric of the church, some final discussion of the building is needed. So far the historical context in which it was built has been summarised, its aesthetic qualities described and the gradual development of the church from east to west set out. Here we need to consider the roles played by the building's patron, the Bishop of Durham, and his master mason, and what sources and influences are evident in the construc-

24 *The west front (left) as it may have appeared around 1175, before the construction of the Galilee chapel and the completion of the western towers (after Curry), and (right) its present appearance*

tion of the church. (This summary draws heavily on recent research noted in the bibliography).

In the high summer of 1093 the foundation stone of Durham Cathedral was laid. The Bishop, William of St Calais, had assembled the nobility of northern Britain for the ceremony. No doubt, his master mason, dubbed the 'First Master' by Ian Curry, the architect of the cathedral, was also in attendance. The bishop, who conceived the vision and paid for the building, and the master mason who realised the vision and produced the detailed design, are the central figures in its creation. Their cathedral church draws on a wide range of cultural sources for its construction. The diversity of such influences only makes the achievement of such a singular and distinctive architectural design all the more exceptional.

The enforced exile of St Calais from 1088-91 must have brought him into direct contact with the great Romanesque churches of France, and possibly, those of other countries further afield. We can see from the evidence of the monastic buildings that his aspirations grew during his absence so that the church as set out after his return, in 1093, was substantially larger than might have been envisaged earlier. The first matter St Calais and his mason had to decide was the size of the building that needed to be laid out on the ground.

It was not uncommon amongst the great Romanesque churches in Europe to seek a direct relationship with the mother church of western Christendom, Old St Peter's in Rome, the early Christian predecessor of the present Renaissance basilica. A number of churches sought a direct dimensional or design link, including Mainz and Speyer Cathedrals in Germany, Pisa Cathedral in Italy, the great abbey church at Cluny and the pilgrimage basilica of St Sernin at Toulouse, the latter two both in France. The external length of Durham Cathedral is 123.09m, Old St Peter's is 122.38m. Similarly its internal width across the choir and aisles relates to the nave width of St Peter's: 23.52m at Durham, 24.71m at St Peter's.

The spiral columns flanking the altar and feretory of the cathedral's east end – the spiritual focus of the building – are related to the spiral columns that once supported the early Christian baldachin around the shrine of St Peter's, spirals being a common late Roman decoration used to signify a special place in a building. The St Peter's baldachin was crowned by open-work ribs and some historians have seen this as explaining the use of rib vaulting to signify a place of importance within the church, such as its eastern bays. These iconic parallels are viewed as St Calais' deliberate wish to associate the northern saint with the greatest of the Apostles, to reflect St Peter's shrine in the monumental architecture around the shrine of St Cuthbert.

The scale and volume of Durham maintain a tradition established by a number of the great English Norman churches, notably St Alban's Abbey (begun 1077), Winchester Cathedral (1079), Ely Cathedral (c.1081), Bury St Edmund's Abbey (c.1081) and Old St Paul's Cathedral in London (after 1087).

These were all pilgrimage churches and their long eastern arms, in contrast to earlier Norman work, were reflected in the new church in Durham. St Alban's in particular also establishes a nave elevation in which the arcade is taller than the gallery, anticipating the Durham treatment. Winchester is influential in the treatment of alternate columnar and compound piers, a device in turn reflecting the nave of Edward the Confessor's Westminster Abbey. Winchester may also have had towers over the eastern bays of its choir aisles and there is strong evidence they existed at Durham as they did at Hereford and Canterbury Cathedrals, originating in earlier German churches.

The very wide spiral staircases in both the western towers and transepts at Durham Cathedral are more common in Norman castles and may have had some military significance in facilitating the movement of troops around the building at high level. Research at Lincoln Cathedral suggests the western end of the building had a military function. Durham, with its generous upper galleries of uncertain function, may well have been more integrated into the network of perimeter walls than has been thought so far. Its position across the body of the peninsula makes contact with the western defences inevitable and, at the very least, the relationship between the castle fortifications and the cathedral church was, perhaps, more interrelated than mutually exclusive.

In the treatment of the cathedral's internal and external arcades a range of influences from Winchester, Normandy and even Islamic Spain have been cited. Durham's distinctive intersecting wall arcading may even be a deliberate Cuthbertian reference to earlier Anglo-Saxon churches. Many of these elements will have been laid down by the bishop in drawing up his brief for the building. The task of the master mason would be to interpret this brief in stone. A number of Anglo-Saxon motifs on the building, linked to a mature knowledge of the great churches of England and Normandy, suggest the 'First Master' may have been English, and possibly trained in the north of England.

The Galilee chapel

The completion of the main body of the cathedral in 1133 provided the bishop and priory with an architectural setting worthy of their great saint. However, paradoxically, despite the church itself being so vast, the circulation of pilgrims around the Shrine of St Cuthbert, confined to the apse behind the high altar, would have been cramped and chaotic.

The problem was finally addressed by Bishop Hugh of Le Puiset in the 1170s. He decided to extend the eastern arm of the church around the shrine, possibly intending to incorporate a Lady Chapel. At each attempt to construct the new work, cracks appeared and the walls collapsed. The tilting geology of the peninsula made the ground at the eastern end of the church less stable than at the west and, when the work was finally abandoned, Le Puiset decided to rebuild his chapel before the west front, perched high above the River Wear. The building was known as the Galilee, the traditional name for the place at the west end of the church where processions end and reassemble before re-entry into the church, as Christ entered Jerusalem from Galilee (**colour plate 9**).

This change of function, which may have included a Lady Altar from its inception, determined the unique five-aisled form of the building. The architecture of the Galilee is transitional between Romanesque and Gothic and, in building it, Le Puiset would have been aware of important contemporary work at York and Winchester that also anticipated the Gothic style. The four-bay arcades that divide the aisles are supported on slender quatrefoil shafts with waterleaf capitals. Originally planned as paired shafts of Purbeck marble, the piers' additional sandstone shafts probably date from the decision to transfer the new work from the east to the west end. Their introduction may have had less to do with structural reinforcement than the reflection of prevailing fashion for quatrefoil piers, which had recently been introduced at York.

If the piers and capitals of the arcade displayed the lightness and simplicity of the emerging Gothic, the arches above held firmly to the late Romanesque tradition, with strongly modelled zigzag ornament. Compare the same zigzag motif on the west front doorway (*c*.1133) to the adjacent Galilee arch (*c*.1175) – in the one decoration is *applied* to the architecture, in the other it has *become* the architecture – a hallmark of late Romanesque ornamentation. Contemporary wall paintings of a King and a bishop in the north-east corner of the Galilee survived the extensive repairs to the chapel's fabric by Bishop Langley in the early fifteenth century. This work significantly remodelled the original Norman form of the building's roofline, replacing three separately high-pitched roofs over nave and inner aisles, with a single shallow pitched roof over the main body of the building. The outer aisles, also shallow roofed by Langley, were probably steeper pitched with individual transverse gables in each bay, an arrangement preserved in the north door, rebuilt in 1863.

The Galilee is a major monument of the late Norman period and represents the turning point in Le Puiset's buildings, by combining the boldness and energy of his late Romanesque work in the castle with the elegance and lightness that was later to develop more fully at Bishop Auckland and Darlington.

The Chapel of the Nine Altars

The completion of the Galilee still did not resolve the pressing problem of St Cuthbert's Shrine, which lacked the space for pilgrims to process and congregate around it. The difficulties at the east end were compounded by the failure of the choir high vault, said to be in danger of collapse in 1235. Furthermore, the growing monastery needed more altars for the individual celebration of the mass. Bishop Richard Poore had planned to extend the church but died before building began in 1242. Though he had founded the great new cathedral at Salisbury, the model for the work at Durham came from much nearer – Fountains Abbey in North Yorkshire.

There, between 1203 and 1247, the Cistercian monks had erected a new east end with an eastern transept or Nine Altars. This innovative architectural design resolved the problems at Durham perfectly. Contemporary eastern extensions at Canterbury and Winchester Cathedrals, also to rehouse their shrines, were inappropriate models for Durham, where the sharply falling land behind the Norman apse would not permit a substantial lengthening of the church.

The Chapel of the Nine Altars at Durham was built to the same ground plan as Fountains and as high as the main church. Work was completed around 1280 (**25**). The construction was of massive proportions, not merely to support its own vaulting but to buttress the entire eastern end of the church. To secure a good foundation required the Chapel to be almost two metres below the level of the choir from which the extended rectangular feretory projected as a raised platform. Inside the Chapel, between its tall lancet windows rose vaulting piers of clustered shafts of Frosterley 'marble', a local limestone from Weardale. The junction with the choir was awkwardly resolved, as the slavish copying of the Fountains' ground plan failed to anticipate the different proportions of the Durham choir and aisles. Consequently, beside the star-shaped central vault, the two flanking vaults are disrupted by large transverse arches cutting arbitrarily across them (**colour plate 11**).

Architectural fashions changed while the building work advanced. The lancet window was outdated by the late thirteenth century and the final modification to the original design was the great north window, the Joseph Window, probably carried out by the wealthy Bishop Bek in the late 1280s. This large traceried composition of intersecting circles marks the point of departure from Early English into the Decorated style. As Pevsner says, 'here richness begins to have precedence over clarity'. Such qualified praise should be set alongside the window's astonishingly advanced structural achievement with its double tracery bracing the vast arched opening.

The fourteenth century

During the century that followed the Joseph Window, there were no major extensions to the fabric of the building, but four additions do echo the 'richness' of the Decorated style and its transformation into the cooler elegance of the Perpendicular. Three of these building projects were undertaken by Prior Fossor, the fourth by Bishop Hatfield, all during the period 1341-81. The earliest is the west window in the nave, the prior's work of around 1341-71, entirely Decorated in spirit with rich flowing tracery in its wide arched head.

25 *The Chapel of the Nine Altars from Kingsgate Bridge.* Royston Thomas

The next addition is the north window in the north transept, an altogether more interesting development. Dating from before 1360, it incorporates, within essentially Decorated tracery, two vertical mullions that strike the main arch without deflection – one of the cardinal marks of Perpendicular architecture and one of its earliest appearances in the north.

Although Bishop Hatfield's Throne and Tomb (1362-81) is an ambitious and unique structure which shows Perpendicular influence, its affinities remain within the more conservative Decorated tradition. The same cannot be said of the nearby Neville Screen. Broadly contemporary with Hatfield's Tomb, it is a work of outstanding quality, almost certainly the masterpiece of the architect Henry Yevele. It served not only as a reredos to the high altar, but also as the façade to the feretory and St Cuthbert's shrine. It was installed in 1380 after being shipped up, piece by piece, from London where it was carved. It is made of Caen stone from Normandy, which allows the most delicate carving. This is the full spirit of the new Perpendicular style with its emphasis on soaring verticality. Five major and four subordinate canopies spire skywards to create a composition in which horizontals are totally suppressed and fragmented. The Screen was painted once and, before the Reformation, it was filled with 107 alabaster figures; but they are scarcely missed.

The towers

Durham Cathedral needs its towers more than most. The church lies in a bowl of rising land and, to the late twelfth-century pilgrim approaching the city, the body of the church would be hidden from view. The form of the Norman central tower that rose above it is unknown. It may have been raised at the same time as the western towers whose upper parts date from the late twelfth and early thirteenth centuries. They exhibit alternating tiers of round and pointed arcades, the latter appropriately used for the structural openings. These towers received timber spires during the thirteenth or fourteenth centuries, possibly original features, though the survival of squinches in the south-west tower suggests that, here at least, a stone spire may have been planned. These spires were removed in 1658 and the present parapets date only from 1801 (**colour plate 8**).

The central tower was rebuilt in the late thirteenth century and repaired after a lightning strike in 1429. When thirty years later lightning struck again, a completely new tower was constructed (*c*.1465-74) complete with crenel-lated parapet (**26**). A second belfry stage was begun around 1483, added on top of the first stage parapet. This was an afterthought as the truncated roof timbers of the tower, completed only a decade before, survive as the gallery of the ringing chamber in the new belfry. This tall tower may be a response to fashion, but it is surely not unconnected with the cathedral's topographical setting deep in its landscape bowl. In the late medieval period, despite the existence of the slender western spires, only the strong silhouette of the tower's upper stage was prominently visible from the surrounding countryside.

The pre-Reformation cathedral

The central tower was the last major new building work on the cathedral, but the completed church as it is seen now would not have been easily recognis-able to the late medieval monastic community. Repairs, refurnishings and

26 *The two-stage, fifteenth-century central tower of the cathedral.* Martin Roberts

restoration after deliberate damage and natural decay have significantly altered the church over the last 350 years. This is particularly true of the interior, whose furnishings have always been a prey to the prevailing liturgical climate as well as a focus for symbolic destruction. Fortunately the pre-Dissolution church has been fully described probably by a former monk of Durham writing in the 1590s (*The Rites of Durham*).

The impression, on the ground at least, would have been one of clutter and subdivision. The great length of the church was broken up by screens and the rood. There were raised lofts in some of the aisles and an abundance of small chapels against walls, between pillars, enclosed in further screenwork. The clarity of the great vista was lacking, substituted by the colour, richness and diversity of the decoration with silver and gilt at every turn. The church would be dark, the light filtering through a wealth of deeply coloured medieval stained glass of which only hundreds of small fragments remain. Colour would

71

be evident on the plastered walls too, which were covered in paintings and decorated with religious iconography.

Nowhere would the contrast with the present have been greater than at the Shrine of St Cuthbert. Nothing, to our eyes, so befits this selfless ascetic as his present plain tombstone. Yet the late medieval monks and benefactors heaped upon his ancient bones a shrine of almost vulgar extravagance – with gilding, painted imagery and a wealth of gifts and jewels displayed in lockers beside the tomb.

John Cosin, prebend and Bishop of Durham

The Reformation brought profound changes to the cathedral. Under the guiding hand of the iconoclast deans, Horne and Whittingham, the church and its shrine were despoiled. Within the nationwide destruction of religious art, the losses at Durham must have been particularly severe. But to the reformers it seemed that they had succeeded in carrying the church forward into the next century, denuded but spiritually cleansed.

Against this puritanical background in the early seventeenth century, Archbishop William Laud led a movement for the restoration of some degree of ritual and ceremony in church services. This movement was called Arminianism, after the writings of a Dutch theologian, and also later became known as the Laudian reforms. It positioned itself at the High Church end of the established church, but the sermons and writings of the Arminians inevitably provoked accusations of 'Popery' from the Low Church puritans. Bishop Richard Neile was an early patron of Laud and during the 1620s he quickly gathered around him like-minded men, including Dean Richard Hunt (installed 1620) and the energetic John Cosin (prebend from 1624). Cosin was Bishop Neile's domestic chaplain and spent much time at Durham House, the bishop's London residence where Neile established the 'Durham House' group of Arminian reformers. Back in Durham it was Hunt and Cosin who began the refurbishment of the cathedral.

The changes that followed finally exasperated the Puritan prebend Peter Smart one Sunday in July 1628. In a spectacular sermon he denounced Cosin for idolatry, 'our young Apollo repaireth the quire, and sets it out gaily, with strange Babylonish ornaments'. The extent of the refurnishings is not known, but something of their character could still be seen in Cosin's work at Brancepeth, where he was the Rector, until the disastrous fire of 1998 utterly destroyed it all. (We must now look at the comparative woodwork in Sedgefield and Haughton-le-Skerne churches for that same spirit and quality.) Smart was jailed for his refusal to recant and released in 1640, when Cosin then stood accused in the changing political and religious climate. Three years later, Cosin fled to Paris to escape further prosecution.

27 *Bishop Cosin's font canopy of 1663.* Royston Thomas

During the turmoil surrounding the Civil War and the Interregnum of the Commonwealth and Protectorate periods, the cathedral again suffered tremendous damage to its interior. The font with its new cover was destroyed by the invading Scots in 1640 during the earlier Bishops' Wars. Ten years later, when they were defeated at the Battle of Dunbar, Cromwell sent back 4,500 Scottish prisoners to England, of whom 3,000 reached Durham and were incarcerated in the cathedral over the winter of 1650-1. Tradition has it that the Scots burnt all the woodwork to keep warm as well as defacing the Neville tombs. This is a debatable point now but, with the Restoration of 1660 and Cosin's triumphant return to Durham as bishop, the church was ripe for an unchallenged refurbishment.

Cosin's woodwork was a synthesis of Gothic and classical forms, the Gothic very much a conscious revival, borrowing motifs from all periods including Norman. The references, particularly in religious work, were obvious; harking back to a pre-Reformation, pre-classical time when the ceremony of church services was marked by lavish decoration and ornament. However, Cosin was no Papist, rather a High Anglican for whom the pomp and ceremony of the liturgy meant much.

The font canopy (1663) is a sensational piece of showmanship, rising from a classical base in keeping with the font itself, hybridising with Gothic forms before ending in its pure Gothic spire. The transition is subtle and symbolic: column to buttress, round arch to pointed, man to God and earth to heaven (**27**). Generally the post-Restoration Cosin work is more baroque in style but the choir stalls, begun 1660, with their high Gothic canopies, may be based on surviving fragments from their medieval predecessors – combining elements of both 'survival' and 'revival'.

Eighteenth and nineteenth centuries

After the dramatic fortunes of the cathedral during the seventeenth century, the years that followed saw no such upheavals. Building work concentrated on the repair and restoration of the medieval fabric, and the different approaches adopted reflected the changing attitudes of both architects and society to the protection of historic monuments. It was not until late in the eighteenth century that the general deterioration in the external fabric was addressed. In 1770 Thomas Wright, the well-known local polymath, first suggested the completion of the towers with pinnacles or 'minarets' as he curiously called them (**28**).

In 1777 John Wooler, a Newcastle surveyor, reported to the dean and chapter on 'the Repairing and Beautifying of the Church', and with his clerk of works, George Nicholson, he supervised work to the Nine Altars and north transept. Later the thirteenth-century north porch was rebuilt to a new design. Most controversially from a modern viewpoint, Wooler recommended the chipping away of the entire external stonework to a depth of up to 3in (75mm) to remove the weathered surfaces. Only where the old churchyard level abutted the church was the original twelfth-century surface preserved below ground. The most accessible section now visible lies due west of the north porch, with more extensive evidence across the churchyard in the angle of the nave and north transept.

In 1795 the eminent architect, James Wyatt, proposed the demolition of the Galilee, to facilitate the opening of the west door, and the removal of both the Neville Screen and the seventeenth-century organ screen. He began work, however, on the Nine Altars where Nicholson's faithful repair work

28 *A mid-eighteenth-century engraving of the cathedral, from the north, showing Thomas Wright's later amendments of 1770, suggesting the restoration of the pinnacles. In the foreground, facing each other across Palace Green, are (left) Bishop Cosin's almshouses, and (right) the gable of the Grammar School and the arcaded County Court or Sessions House.* Durham Cathedral

was undone, restoring the original lancets, redesigning the rose window and refacing the whole façade. These 'improvements' infuriated John Carter of the Society of Antiquaries, who attacked him in articles in *The Gentleman's Magazine*. Public protest was so great that the Galilee demolition was abandoned and Wyatt departed in 1797, leaving the resident cathedral architect, Morpeth, in charge. The adverse publicity did not prevent all demolition and in 1801-2 the late thirteenth-century revestry against the south choir aisle was swept away. Wright and Wooler's original suggestion that the western towers be restored with battlements and pinnacles was finally executed around 1801.

In 1804 the local architect William Atkinson proposed the use of Parker's Cement in the repair of mouldings and decayed stonework on the central tower. The work was stopped in 1808 when the chapter felt unhappy with the results. Atkinson was paid off but his importance lies in his appreciation of the building's patina, against the prevailing climate for wholesale renewal. The general stone work repairs were continuing on the south side of the church, where Morpeth had completed the Nine Altars' south-east turret in 1812-3.

In 1827 the locally renowned architect, Ignatius Bonomi, undertook to continue the work, restoring the Nine Altar's south-west turret and south wall, where he ignored Wyatt's plan and retained the later tracery in the lancets. Bonomi's work here, and moving round the church to the south transept, is characterised by his use of a golden brown sandstone, in marked contrast to the later south side refacing by cathedral architects, George Jackson and George Pickering in the 1840s, working under Anthony Salvin, who employed a grey and dullish sandstone from Gateshead Fell.

Salvin and Pickering together supervised the reordering of the Cathedral interior between 1844 and 1849. This included relocating the Cosin font, Prior Castell's clock and widening the choir by cutting up the Cosin stalls and placing them *between* the choir piers. They also relocated the organ to the north side of the choir and removed Cosin's choir screen at the crossing, thus creating an uninterrupted 'grand vista' the length of the church. In the repair of windows, there was a return to the Wyatt approach of restoring the original Norman designs, ignoring Bonomi's enlightened work in the Nine Altars, and only the west face of the north transept escaped with its tracery intact.

In 1860 the restoration of the central tower was carried out by the new consultant, George Gilbert Scott. He also reintroduced the principle of a Choir Screen with a bold new design six years later, when the novelty of the 'grand vista' had worn off and some re-emphasis of the choir's separateness was needed. He also restored the Cosin stalls to their original position. The clerk of works during much of Scott's consultancy was E.R. Robson, who supervised repairs at the west end of the church and was a founder member of the Society for the Protection of Ancient Buildings. His successor Charles Hodgson Fowler carried out perhaps the last full-blooded restoration in the rebuilding of the Norman chapter house in 1895. Since then, repairs have proceeded with greater emphasis on the retention of as much of the original fabric as possible, but with equal design skill evident in the execution of new work, furnishings and fittings.

The development of the monastic buildings

When Bishop Walcher (1071-80) decided to regularise the Anglo-Saxon community, his first priority was to renew their accommodation. The existing Anglo-Saxon church would have been sufficiently large to continue in use, while the traditional ranges of monastic buildings were constructed around three sides of a cloister, with the church against the fourth, northern side.

Walcher began with the east range which provided the principal domestic and administrative accommodation in the monastery. At the time of his murder in 1080, he had most probably constructed the chapter house and the central section of the dormitory undercroft. St Calais continued the work, completing the ground floor and finishing the dormitory over the whole range, certainly by the time of his exile in 1088, and possibly as early as 1083, when the Benedictine monks were installed.

During St Calais' exile the monks are said to have constructed the refectory in the south range. They probably also established the west wall of the cloister. On his return, St Calais implemented his great plan for the new cathedral church which far exceeded the plan anticipated by Walcher when he set out the first monastic buildings. Clearly the cloister would need enlarging (**29**). Little is known of the monastic buildings during the construction of the cathedral, and it could be assumed that every effort was directed towards the church's construction to the detriment of further work around the cloister. It is clear that the first dormitory was linked to the new church via a night stair in the south transept, as suggested by an opening in the present Song School, over the slype. Probably, when work was nearing completion on the nave around 1130, it was decided to rebuild the chapter house on a scale befitting the new church. This new building, with its high-ribbed vaulting, was completed by Bishop Rufus and cut through the dormitory, thereby denying direct access to the church. Between 1144 and 1152, St Barbara rebuilt it in the west range of the newly enlarged cloister, taking advantage of the adjacent riverbanks to provide greatly improved sanitation for the growing monastery. At the same time the south range was extended westwards to meet it (**21**). Into the thirteenth century, this move westwards continued with the construction of the large aisled halls of the infirmary and guest hall.

The old dormitory was given over to the prior for his lodgings, and these were extended eastwards sufficiently for a chapel to be added in about 1244. At about the same time St Barbara's dormitory was rebuilt on its present plan and a new octagonal laver in the cloister was built to replace the late twelfth-century one opposite the refectory door. The history of the later medieval priory buildings is one of replacement, enlargement and improvement. The prior's lodgings were rebuilt in the mid-fourteenth century and the great kitchen constructed. The dormitory was rebuilt for a fourth time and in the early fifteenth century a spate of major buildings was undertaken – the cloisters, a new library, the infirmary and more work in the prior's lodgings. Finally, in the early sixteenth century, the priory gateway and the service buildings along the eastern side of the outer court were rebuilt.

The cloisters and claustral ranges

The present cloisters represent the enlarged monastic plan, established in response to the new cathedral church in 1093 (**21**). Le Puiset (1153-95) is credited with their construction, late in his episcopate. They were rebuilt in

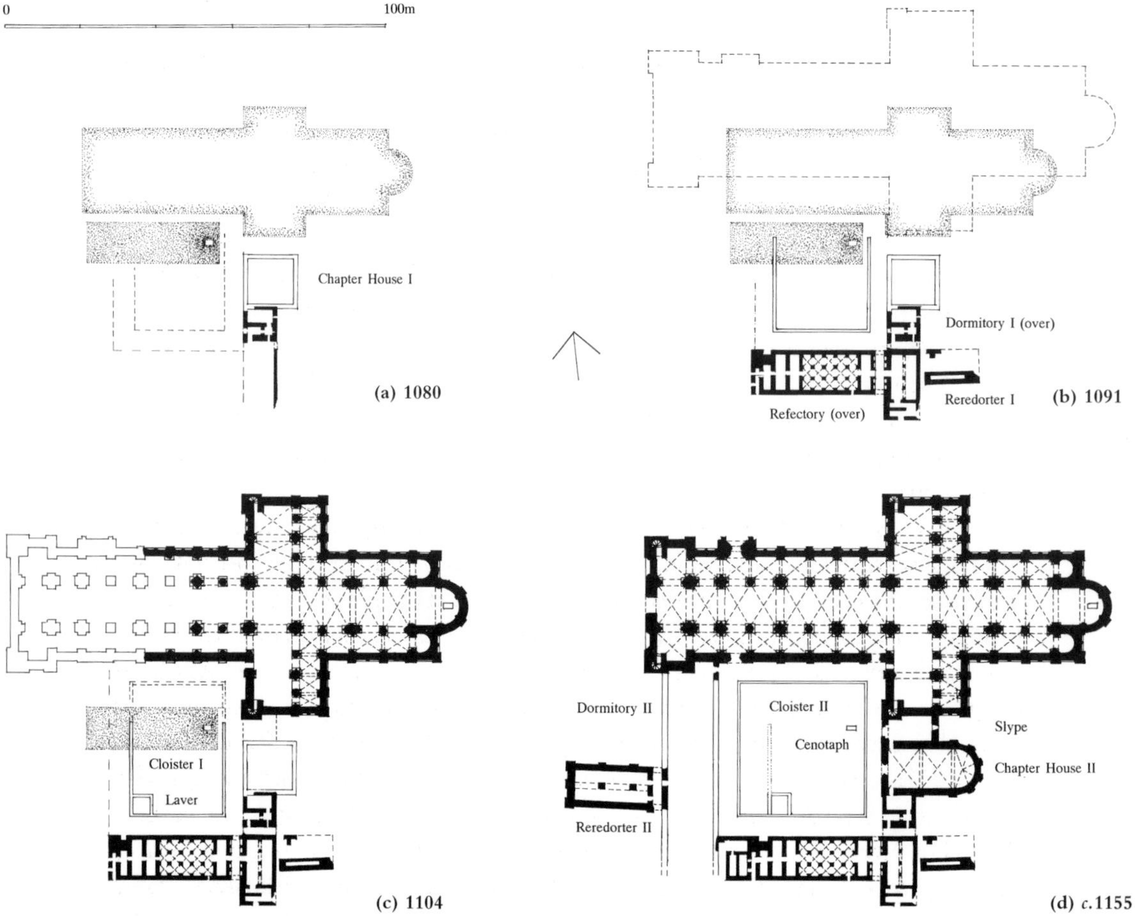

0   100m

Chapter House I

(a) 1080

Dormitory I (over)

Refectory (over)   Reredorter I   (b) 1091

Cloister I

Laver

(c) 1104

Dormitory II   Cloister II   Slype

Cenotaph   Chapter House II

Reredorter II

(d) c.1155

29 *The development of the Norman cathedral and priory: (a) Walcher's work in the east range, south-east of the Anglo-Saxon church, up to his death in 1080. The stippled area identifies the suggested general position of the main body of this church, with St Cuthbert's tomb at its head (after Briggs, Cambridge and Bailey). This conjectural development assumes the existence of a single Anglo-Saxon church. The stippled outline suggests the general scale only of the first Norman church that Walcher, or perhaps St Calais, intended should replace the Anglo-Saxon church, once the claustral ranges were complete. It was never built. (b) St Calais continued with the monastic buildings and the monks themselves constructed the south range before his return from exile in 1091. The west wall of the cloister was constructed in anticipation of the final monastic plan with the smaller church. (c) This plan was abandoned in favour of a much larger church and, by 1104, the great Norman cathedral was sufficiently complete in its eastern parts to enable the translation of St Cuthbert's body and the demolition of the remains of the Anglo-Saxon church. (d) By around 1155 the church had been completed, the chapter house rebuilt and the cloisters enlarged with the extended south range and the construction of a new dormitory and reredorter in the west range*

the early fifteenth century in their present form, with the severe tracery substituted in a restoration of 1764-9.

The east range of the monastic buildings is full of contrasts, brought about by the radical change in St Calais' plans. Beforehand, in 1088, he was content to continue building modestly enough on Walcher's work at the southern end of the range, identified by the curiously irregular rubble walling visible in the cloisters. The later doorway led to the day stairs up to the dormitory over the whole range. Beneath these stairs are three small chambers used in late medieval times as a prison for minor offenders. After his return in 1091, St Calais set out the great church, thereby committing his successors, Flambard and Rufus, to the same vision. As the church neared completion, the inadequacy of the priory's chapter house would have been woefully apparent. The chapter house was the focal point of the monastic buildings, the centre for the daily administration of the priory. It demanded a material expression worthy of its status.

It was completed between 1133 and 1141, an imposing room with its zigzag ornament on arches and vaulting ribs, and its fine entrance portal with richly carved capitals. Its eastern apse, and all of its vaulting, was removed in 1796, but the restoration of 1895 kept close to the original plan and utilised original fragments. The vaulting ribs in the apse were supported on atlantes – sculpted male figures used instead of columns – a motif unique in England and probably derived indirectly from examples in northern Italy and the south of France. The originals are now reset in the north wall. The chapter house also served as a burial place for the Norman bishops and, despite its largely Victorian interior, it is a rare feeling to stand in the exalted (or notorious?) company of St Calais, Flambard and Le Puiset. One final addition to the range was the construction of the library, begun in 1414-5. It was situated over the slype and its traceried windows were later restored by Bonomi.

The south range of a Benedictine monastery was devoted to the preparation and consumption of food: so it was in Durham. The first early Norman refectory (c.1088-91) was raised over the surviving plain, groin-vaulted undercroft. It is separated from the similar undercroft in the east range by a tunnel-vaulted passage, which gave access to the outer court. At the Reformation, the refectory became the petty canons hall, but by 1665 was 'useless and ruined'. Its conversion by Dean Sudbury into a library raised a new floor high above its medieval predecessor, so preserving part of its early sixteenth-century tiled floor, the eleventh-century dais steps and the suggestion of a large oriel window to light the dais. On the library's east wall important Romanesque wall paintings are preserved behind later panelling.

By the late medieval period, the refectory was only used by the whole community on special feast days. Usually the senior monks ate in a room at the west end of the south range known as the Loft, a portion of the original western extension of the range added as part of the enlarged cloisters.

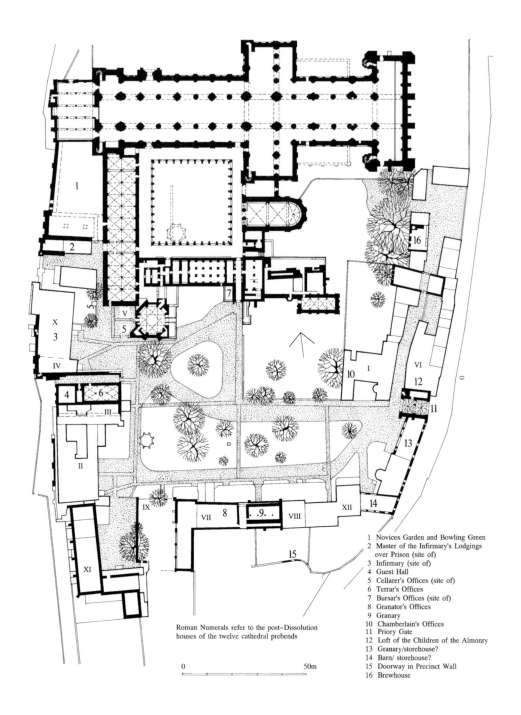

1 Novices Garden and Bowling Green
2 Master of the Infirmary's Lodgings
  over Prison (site of)
3 Infirmary (site of)
4 Guest Hall
5 Cellarer's Offices (site of)
6 Terrar's Offices
7 Bursar's Offices (site of)
8 Granator's Offices
9 Granary
10 Chamberlain's Offices
11 Priory Gate
12 Loft of the Children of the Almonry
13 Granary/storehouse?
14 Barn/ storehouse?
15 Doorway in Precinct Wall
16 Brewhouse

Roman Numerals refer to the post–Dissolution
houses of the twelve cathedral prebends

0   50m

30 *The plan of the priory showing the known medieval buildings. (Significant remains of medieval date, as yet not fully recorded, are to be found in most of the present college buildings.)*

Dean Sudbury's new library grew out of the shell of the monastic refectory and was begun during his period of office (1662–84) but only completed after his death. It seems to have been one of those awkward equivocal classical and Gothic designs that probably contented its builders, intrigues present day architectural historians, but infuriated the Victorian purists. The conversion of the refectory, and later petty canons' hall, incorporated a fine classical doorway in the cloister and major refenestration and recladding of the north and south walls, with semicircular headed openings, maintaining, it seems, the classical theme throughout. In the event, a weak tracery was installed within the openings and the walls crowned with a crenellated parapet, a mixture of styles that frequently found favour in the seventeenth century. Such architectural ambiguities were anathema to the restoration architects of the Victorian period. Salvin's remodelling of the building in the 1850s completely removed any shadow of stylistic doubt by inserting faithful Perpendicular windows and correcting the parapet (**colour plate 10**). Could this be another instance of Cosin, or even Crewe, influencing the design halfway through? Might they have accepted the cloister door but insisted that the wider view of the claustral buildings should retain a wholly medieval appearance? Salvin's enthusiasm for correctness may well have also led to the removal of the charming eighteenth-century Gothic design for the adjacent Butler's pantry in the deanery, probably swept away in the same contract as the library.

The monks' laver stood in the cloister garth opposite the refectory door. The thirteenth-century octagonal design was said in *The Rites* to be all of marble, 'save the verie uttermost walls', with brass fittings, seven windows and a dovecot on top. Its central basin of Egglestone 'marble' was made in 1432-3 and now stands in the middle of the garth. The 'Great Kitchen' (1366-74) is one of the most important monastic buildings in England (**colour plate 12**). It served not only the refectory and Loft but also the prior's lodgings, and possibly the guest hall and infirmary too, centrally located between them all (**31**).

The master mason in charge was John Lewyn and, though his spectacular eight-cornered star-vault is said to be influenced by Muslim vaults of southern Spain, it is more likely to be a brilliant engineering response to providing a fireproof roof with a central louvre in an octagonal building. The west range of the enlarged cloister was established in the mid-twelfth century with the construction of the new dormitory, removed from the east range. The doorway into the cloisters adjoining the south-west tower survives from that period, as well as some of the masonry abutting the reredorter. The mid-thirteenth century rebuilding established the present plan of an undercroft of twelve double bays of quadripartite vaulting. This subvault was later divided up into, from the north, a treasury, a common or warming house – originally the only room in the monastery with a fire – a passage to the infirmary and, in the southern four bays, a great cellar or buttery, where the present restaurant is situated.

Above this undercroft the dormitory was rebuilt in 1398-1404 on an impressive scale (**32**). It was originally partitioned into a series of cubicles, each with its own window low down, while in the wall above, wider-spaced windows lit the whole interior. The magnificent roof, rough and robust yet also delicately cusped along the underside of its ridge beam, is the work of Ellis Harpour, who obtained the timber from the prior, including 21 massive tie beams, each over 12.3m (41ft) in length.

The original twelfth-century reredorter survived until the late eighteenth century. Now its west wall remains within the peninsula defences and its southern boundary survives as the north wall of later stables, now public toilets, which stand on the site of the Master of the Infirmary's lodgings. Deep beneath its floor is a high cavernous chamber abutting the lowest offset plinths of the reredorter, its tunnel-vault springing from short columns and shallow segmental arches. Its use is far from certain. It is sometimes called the 'Lying

31 *The prior's kitchen, when still used to serve the deanery in 1911. From* The Story of the Deanery *by Dean G.W. Kitchin*

32 *Interior of the dormitory showing the great roof of 1398-1404.* North East Civic Trust

House' but more commonly named the monastic prison, a use that seems increasingly improbable to many scholars.

The deanery

The deanery was formerly the prior's lodgings. Originally the prior had only a bed in the communal dormitory, in strict observance of the Benedictine rule. However, when the monks moved to the west range, he no doubt took the old dormitory as his lodgings and, over the centuries, successive deans have developed them into the lavish suite of rooms that remains. It serves as a fitting metaphor for both the general development of English Benedictine monasticism and the particular importance of the prior of Durham. Here is a denial of the simple contemplative life of the religious ascetic and an acknowledgement of the power and wealth of one of the great feudal overlords of the region.

From the old dormitory, the prior's lodgings extended east incorporating the remains of the first reredorter. In the mid-thirteenth century the prior's chapel was built, further to the east, raised over the surviving vaulted under-croft (**33**). The chapel itself, now with an inserted floor and subdivided, had lancet windows and was approached via some form of external stair to its west door. Inside fine fifteenth-century wall paintings were recently discovered.

83

33 *The deanery from the south-west with the main fourteenth-century chambers (left) and beyond, the converted mid-thirteenth-century chapel with the surviving lancets on its west front.* Royston Thomas

The central range between the chapel and east range of the cloister was rebuilt in the fourteenth century and comprised an upper and lower chamber, linked by a staircase in a projecting turret on the south wall. Perhaps a little later the range of private apartments extended to the north-east.

Prior John Wessington (1416-46) spent the huge sum of over £400 on the building described as 'greatly ruined' in 1416. He constructed the north range and improved the whole suite of rooms. Later, in the fifteenth and sixteenth centuries, low-pitched roofs were provided over the great chamber, the east range rooms, and over the prior's hall. Some are still visible and others are occasionally glimpsed above later ceilings, such as that in the great chamber. During post-Dissolution alterations, the chapel roof was also replaced by one of a shallower pitch. Little is known about these works. Much of the architecture is of eighteenth-century date whilst documents speak of Dean Comber (1671-9) 'very much improving' the deanery. A major repair was carried out in 1971 (**33**).

The College

The College is the former outer court of the monastery, known in the sixteenth century as the Abbey Garth. At the Dissolution it was converted into accommodation for the dean and the twelve new prebends of the Durham chapter. It is one of the most private and tranquil places in the city, a picturesque assemblage of stone and slate around its central lawns. Sadly this idyllic visual appeal has misled even the most respected of recent commentators into dismissing its buildings as of no intrinsic interest. This is a great mistake.

What has emerged in recent years is a growing body of evidence to suggest that, despite the preponderance of Georgian façades and the claims of seventeenth-century prebends to wholesale rebuilding, much of the fabric of the College buildings is that of the medieval monastery. The evidence is sometimes well concealed and fragmented by later work, but all deserving of much closer study. The history of the College houses, therefore, remains to be written. What then is known?

The group comprises ranges on the south, east and west sides. The west range overlooked the steep riverbanks and has become incorporated into the peninsula defences (**19**). The line of the castle wall may have shifted west here during the twelfth century to accommodate the considerable pressure for new buildings that took place in the area. This was perhaps generated by the transfer of the dormitory to the west range in the middle of the century and the very considerable advantages to be gained from buildings that could be drained easily onto the river banks. As a consequence the large aisled infirmary, a vast communal hall more usually located east of the east range, occupied a mirrored position west of the west range. This building, probably of early thirteenth century date, was pressed hard against the castle wall. The position of two of its arcade piers is known and indicates a building of at least seven bays in length. In common with most monastic infirmaries, this building would have been subdivided and remodelled in the later medieval period to create more private and discrete apartments for the monks. The present cellular structure may well incorporate the core of the earlier communal hall, and later medieval remains are certainly visible in numbers 13, 14 and 15, despite major alterations made in the late seventeenth to early eighteenth centuries and in the early nineteenth century. In its original form the infirmary would have had its own chapel and kitchen, though the latter may have moved into the great kitchen in the later fourteenth century. This kitchen may also have provided food for the other great outer court building constructed here, the guest hall.

This hall stood south of the infirmary and, according to *The Rites*, 'This haule is a goodly brave place, much like unto the body of a Church, with very fair pillars supporting yt on ether syde, and in the mydest of the haule a most large rannge for the fyer'. This aisled hall, probably of five bays, stood where

the later prebendal houses (numbers 12 & 13) were built and its fine thirteenth-century vaulted undercroft survives from beneath the eastern part of
the hall. Under its north aisle runs the passage and postern leading out to the
riverbanks, known as the Dark Entry. Further south the buildings of the
Choristers' School (numbers 9 & 10) incorporate medieval work in the long
range against the castle walls and in the block at right angles that now faces the
vestiges of Dr Pickering's gardens and fountain (1689-1710).

The south range comprised four prebendal houses of which one, at the west
end, was demolished around 1840. Nevertheless, in the remnants of walling on
the open site is a thirteenth-century lancet window. Overlooking this gap, on
the east side, within the rear wing of number 8, is an imposing three-bay
arcade of the same date incorporated in the west wall. The original form and
function of this building is unknown.

The centre of the south range retains its medieval plan intact, as the
surviving buttresses indicate, despite being swamped in Georgian doors and
windows. According to *The Rites*, the monastic granaries were here, together
with the offices of the granator – the monk responsible for obtaining wheat,
barley and malt, etc. for the priory. Number 6 incorporates a tunnel-vaulted
passage under the range with a vaulted undercroft on its east side. Number 5
(Department of Palaeography), though repaired in the seventeenth and early
eighteenth century was almost entirely reconstructed around 1812, but retains
medieval work in its basement. Rebuilt during the early nineteenth-century
fashion for stucco and render, the exposed walls of number 5 were clearly
never meant to be seen. One day they may return to their 'natural' state.

The east range comprised predominantly service buildings in medieval
times, and consequently only two properties were converted into prebendal
houses at the Dissolution. Later conversions occurred (numbers 2-4) south of
the gatehouse and number 4, for example, grew out of a small barn. The group
of modest buildings up the little cobbled lane north of College Gate also
includes important medieval survivals. Most significant is the brewhouse, with
a massive chimney stack, brick-lined vat and original stone flagged floor.
Spanning the lane is the present timber loft, a stone-walled service building
with substantial timber framing and brick infilling. The atmosphere of clutter
and activity found here in this treeless gravelled yard is perhaps more redolent
of the whole outer court's medieval appearance than the present College's
manicured lawns.

Opposite the yard entrance by College gate is number 16/16A, one of the
College's prettiest houses and formerly the Chamberlain's Exchequer, an
administrative building belonging to one of the priory's many officers or
obedientaries. The similarity of its present form to a medieval hall and cross
wings is perhaps misleading, but there are significant medieval features inside
that need explaining. The main section of the east range appears to have
undergone major rebuilding in the years before the Dissolution. The priory

gatehouse was rebuilt around 1500 by Prior Castell, with St Helen's Chapel above it (**34**). This gateway must have replaced an earlier entrance and the large thirteenth-century arches in the basement of the adjoining building to the north may be related to this earlier gate. This building was known as the 'Loft of the Children of the Almonry' according to *The Rites*.

South of the gatehouse, the rebuilding continued with the construction of the large service building around 1531-2 above the earlier precinct wall (numbers 1/2). This building may have extended along the whole range as indicated by the external string course. Raised over a basement, its main floor had three basket-arched openings facing into the court. Its function is unknown; yet another granary or storehouse seems likely. Inside its original roof survives, a truncated principal truss design in which the shortened principal rafters are linked by a collar below the apex of the roof. This design reoccurs in the cathedral's north transept (*c*.1458), Elvethall Manor (*c*.1466) and Crook Hall (*c*.1468).

The design also appears in the most modest of the College houses – number 4, recently tree-ring dated to around 1445. This was formerly a small barn or store, with triangular ventilation slits beside wide opposed doors. It was

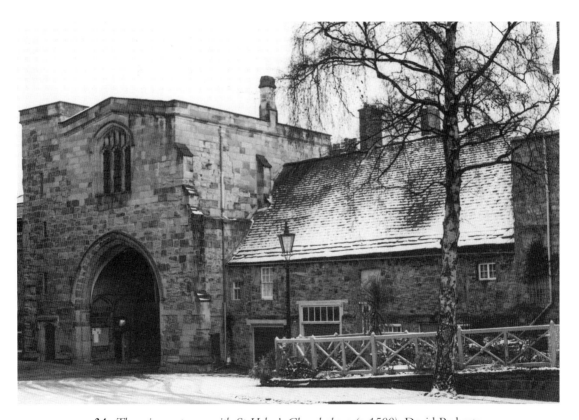

34 *The priory gateway, with St Helen's Chapel above (c.1500).* David Roberts

shortened by the rebuilding of number 5 and masked by the gable of number 3, yet still manages to steal a little light from its overbearing neighbours. From the east gable of number 4 the monastic, in part still medieval, precinct wall stretches away southwards around St Mary-the-Less, heading west towards the castle wall.

4

THE MEDIEVAL TOWN

At the end of the twelfth century the fortified peninsula at Durham was a citadel – an exclusive concentration of religious and political power. Within its castle walls lay the bishop's palace and his cathedral church. Between them were laid out around Palace Green the courts, exchequer and other great offices from which the bishop wielded his temporal power over much of Northumbria. Beyond the cathedral lay the Benedictine monastery, the successor of the Community of St Cuthbert and custodian of his shrine. After the bishop, the priory was the greatest landowner of the palatinate and a major influence on the life of the city. Beside their great buildings lay the dwellings of the palatine officials and the castle garrison in the outer bailey.

To have walked the streets of this citadel, as the contemporary chroniclers Laurence and Reginald have described, was to walk in a fortress town. Wherever one travelled, one had to pass through walls, beneath watching guards. There would have been no shops, no markets; they lay outside the walls. It would have been a busy place with its garrison, clerics and officials: there would be the steady stream of pilgrims and, as Laurence recalls in a poetic counterpoint to the monolithic permanence of church and castle, there was the laughter of children at play on Palace Green.

This core of power, this command centre, was not self-supporting. Durham's success as a religious and political capital lay as much in its ability to develop a community that serviced these two great institutions as in the institutions themselves. The third element in the sustaining power of Durham was the medieval town.

The establishment of the medieval town

There is a general recognition that the Community of St Cuthbert did not stumble on the peninsula by accident in 995, but moved to it when the place had been prepared in advance as a fortified site to receive the precious relic of the saint's body. There may well have been an earlier settlement but as yet there is no reliable evidence for any human activity there that can be securely dated before the Community's arrival. Durham was established in an area of existing small agricultural settlements that could supply the fledgling religious community and its military protectors with food and provisions. A market developed as local inhabitants diversified from agriculture into specialist trades and service industries to meet the town's needs. With Durham as the focus for their goods, villagers would have moved to the town to develop their market.

Archaeological excavations in Saddler Street, outside the fortified peninsula, have revealed timber buildings from about the year 1000. These structures, lying parallel to the street, housed a shoemaker, cobbler, turner of wooden bowls, potter, butcher and fishmonger: the typical components of the service economy established from the earliest years of the city. Significantly, despite the physical upheavals of the Norman reordering of Durham and the realignment of narrow tenements with buildings end on to the street, independent craftsmen and tradesmen remained on the site throughout the Norman occupation. The shoe-making business in particular continued without a break into the late twelfth and early thirteenth centuries.

The focus of their activity would be the market place, where traders met their military and religious clients. It was once assumed that in Saxon and early Norman times this lay within the fortifications where Palace Green now stands, between the castle and the cathedral. There is however a compelling argument that to allow an open market accessible to all and sundry within the heart of the fortified area would have been foolish and dangerous. In keeping with other military strongholds, the original market may well have developed roughly on the site of the present Market Place outside the walls.

Durham offered not only a livelihood to local traders but also security against Danish, and later, Scottish raids. The protection provided by the bishop's castle and its garrison to the surrounding population in times of strife would have encouraged the development of trade. That trade might have led to even greater expansion had communications been better, but the self-imposed isolation of the founders of the city on their 'hill-island' did necessitate the development of settlements on neighbouring river banks, and this led to the gradual creation of the city's unique plan.

Development of the medieval town

The town plan of Durham was largely established by around 1250. It altered little during the succeeding 600 years, only expanding significantly in the nineteenth century (**35**). One of its most distinctive features was its subdivision into separate parts. There was the fortified peninsula encompassing castle, cathedral and priory. Then there were four areas called 'boroughs': the Old Borough, the Bishop's Borough, Elvet Borough and St Giles Borough. The sixth part was the Barony of Elvet. The ownership and administration of

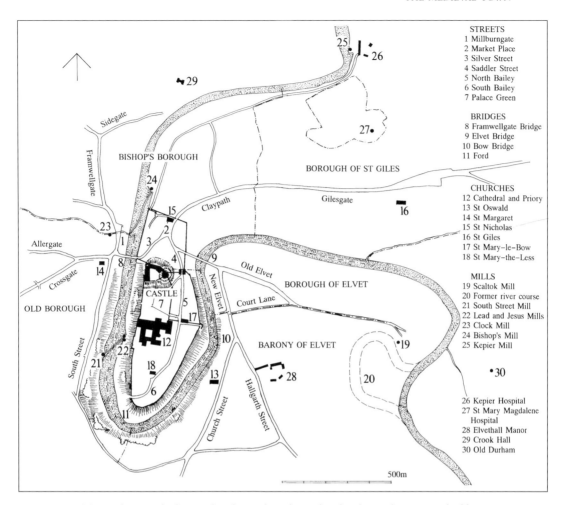

STREETS
1 Millburngate
2 Market Place
3 Silver Street
4 Saddler Street
5 North Bailey
6 South Bailey
7 Palace Green

BRIDGES
8 Framwellgate Bridge
9 Elvet Bridge
10 Bow Bridge
11 Ford

CHURCHES
12 Cathedral and Priory
13 St Oswald
14 St Margaret
15 St Nicholas
16 St Giles
17 St Mary–le–Bow
18 St Mary–the–Less

MILLS
19 Scaltok Mill
20 Former river course
21 South Street Mill
22 Lead and Jesus Mills
23 Clock Mill
24 Bishop's Mill
25 Kepier Mill

26 Kepier Hospital
27 St Mary Magdalene Hospital
28 Elvethall Manor
29 Crook Hall
30 Old Durham

500m

35 *Durham in the late medieval period: its boroughs, churches and important buildings*

these areas originated with the bishop. When St Calais established the Benedictine monastery in 1083, he endowed the new priory with substantial portions of his palatinate estates including the Old Borough and the Barony of Elvet. In due course Kepier Hospital received the Borough of St Giles from Bishop Le Puiset.

The castle area, incorporating the whole of the fortifications, was administered on behalf of the bishop by a constable. Across the river to the east, the Barony of Elvet developed from the early settlement that probably grew up around St Oswald's Church prior to the arrival of the monks in 995. Fordable in places from the peninsula, it would have been a valuable foothold on the opposite bank of the Wear. Its main street was Old Elvet (now New Elvet) and later expanded into Church Street and Hallgarth Street, where stood the priory's Elvethall Manor. The main north-south route through the palatinate passed the peninsula on its western side along the present line of

South Street-Milburngate-Framwellgate. Here was the Old Borough, probably an early trading place in the eleventh century. From its centre, Crossgate led out to Brancepeth in the west with smaller Alvertongate (now Allergate) branching off it.

Around the year 1120, Bishop Flambard constructed the Old Bridge, now Framwellgate Bridge, to link the old market area with the new street of the same name, a detached development in his newly founded Bishop's Borough. From the Market Place, Clayport (now Claypath) ran north–north–east and became St Giles Street (now Gilesgate) leading to Sherburn and Pittington. Silver Street dropped down to the Old Bridge while Fleshewergate (now Fleshergate) and Sadler Gate (now Saddler Street) ran south to the castle's North Gate. The increased east-west traffic that would be encouraged by the construction of the Old Bridge led logically to the building of the New Bridge (Elvet Bridge) by Bishop Le Puiset (1153-95) and the establishment of a new Borough of Elvet covering the principal street of New Elvet (now Old Elvet). The new borough was given to the priory, its boundary with the Barony being Ratonrawe (now Court Lane) which used to lead to the important Scaltock Mills.

St Giles Borough grew up around the hospital of St Giles, established by Bishop Flambard in 1112. The hospital was refounded around 1180 by Le Puiset at Kepier, following the destruction of St Giles in the Cumin rebellion in 1144. The bishop gave the Borough to the hospital as part of its estate. An area around St Mary Magdalene's chapel remained in the hands of the priory. The boroughs were independent urban communities with their own churches, courts and mills, and maintained their separate identities to the end of the medieval period. Though the priory held three boroughs, the Bishop's Borough was the only one with a market, and the bishop fought hard to maintain this considerable advantage. In their origins as independent single street settlements, they are distinctive from the more usual suburban ribbon development of medieval towns that fan out along radial routes. That more common characteristic is evident in the later stages of Durham borough development when the separate settlements had begun to coalesce.

The buildings of the town

To present a balanced picture of the medieval town based only on surviving buildings would be a gross distortion. A great deal has been lost over the centuries. Archival and archaeological evidence is needed to supplement the meagre and unrepresentative medieval architecture that still stands, predominantly the parish churches. Of its secular public buildings there are no remains from any of the six boroughs. The town's domestic buildings have fared little better, though examples cloaked in later fabric are coming to light.

The bridges

The River Wear was, and remains today, one of the greatest influences on the city. The peninsula's isolation encouraged development on opposite river banks and these developments proceeded for probably a hundred years with only fordable crossing places and ferries to link the communities. By the time the bridges were built, the distinctive development of the separate communities was well advanced. The river, though shallow, was prone to rise swiftly in bad weather and in medieval times there was disastrous flooding on several occasions. The Elvet Borough was particularly badly hit and in the fifteenth century a river wall was constructed there to prevent repetition. The townspeople did not use the river for drinking water. Wells and piped water, carried to the peninsula by lead pipes, provided the necessary supply. More conveniently, the river served the town as an open sewer.

Framwellgate Bridge (the 'Old Bridge') was built around 1120 by Bishop Flambard to link the two halves of his Borough and the Old Borough. The bridge is thought to have had at least four arches. It was positioned close to the castle so it could be defended, with some facility for the castle garrison to gain easy access and may have incorporated gatehouses and other fortifications from the start. In a flood in 1400 the bridge was swept away but was soon rebuilt by Bishop Langley with two very wide elliptical arches and gate towers at each end. Watercolour paintings by Turner, Cotman and Girton (c.1787-1806) reveal a third semi-circular land arch on the peninsula, possibly a survivor of Flambard's bridge. The arch was still visible early last century and presumably still survives beneath the carriageway.

The bridge was a vital link between the commercial centre of medieval Durham around the Market Place and the wider countryside beyond, and would also have catered for the growing number of pilgrims to the shrine of St Cuthbert. Merchants and craftsmen, keen to capture the passing trade, gained consent to build shops and booths off the bridge structure, ensuring free access along its narrow roadway. The land arches and abutments were heavily cluttered in the medieval period and by the late sixteenth century, if not earlier, the central abutment had been built on too. The combination of gate towers and commercial encroachment eventually led to the passage over the bridge being badly restricted. The decline of Durham's defensive role and the demand for a more commodious approach to the peninsula led to the removal of all fortifications by about 1760, the eastern gate tower being the last to go. Properties adjacent to the bridge were being acquired under the 1790 Durham Paving Act and acquisitions were still being made in 1828. The long-awaited widening scheme was finally executed on the south side in 1859.

If Framwellgate Bridge was Durham's first river crossing, the construction, by Bishop Le Puiset, of Elvet Bridge (the 'New Bridge') at the end of the twelfth century, probably after 1170 and before 1195, was significant for being

36 *Elvet Bridge in the third quarter of the eighteenth century, from the north, before widening. Beyond, on the peninsula, the North Gate and castle keep still stand complete. Behind 41/42 Saddler Street the theatre building, with its two rows of four windows, can be seen clearly.* Private collection print from an original by Thomas Hearne in Leeds City Art Gallery

a far more ambitious project. The bridge was built to link the Market Place to the important boroughs in Elvet, joining the Priory to its Elvethall Manor estate. It provided the entrance to the east side of the city as Framwellgate Bridge did on the west (**36**). It was a very long sloping structure, rising from the flood plain on the Elvet side to join the peninsula at a high level on Saddler Street. Its lengthy flank was overlooked by the North Gate and the north-east corner of the castle walls where Le Puiset's rebuilding incorporated a large turret, still extant. The bridge ran to the south of an ancient vennel from Saddler Street down to the river, said to be the route to the old ford.

Le Puiset's bridge may not have lasted long. In 1225 the Archbishop of York issued indulgences for those contributing to the construction of 'the new bridge of Elvete at Durham', presumably in response to possible flood damage. Whether the bridge was substantially repaired or completely rebuilt, we do not know. After 1315 the bridge was incorporated into the new town walls with a gate and tower built at the west end. Two chantry chapels were built on the bridge. The first, St Andrew's, at the east end on the south side, was established (or perhaps re-established) between 1274 and 1283 by William, son of Absalon. The second, St James', at the west end, was founded in the late thirteenth century by a butcher, Thomas, son of Lewyn. The chantries shared a chaplain, for some time during the fourteenth century. At the Dissolution of the chantry chapels in the mid-sixteenth century, the relative sizes of the buildings are helpfully indicated by the calculation of their lead roofing – 36 square yards at St James' and 88 square yards at St Andrew's.

Like Framwellgate Bridge, Elvet Bridge's prime location for trading encouraged building upon, beside and overhanging the bridge structure. Indeed the scope for innovative commercial development was far greater on the longer and more complex Elvet Bridge and may even have extended to spanning across the old vennel leading down to the river on the north side. Booths are mentioned in the priory accounts around 1348 and such was the pressure for development in the early fifteenth century that, while the outer parts of the city declined, the Almoner of the priory subdivided one of his tenements into four parts and almost trebled his income. At the end of the fourteenth century the chaplain of St James leased two land arches at the end of his chapel, probably for storage.

The concentration of buildings continued with the establishment of the House of Correction in 1632 on the north side of the peninsula end of the bridge, beside the vennel. Innovative trading positions continued to be seized as in 1662 when Henry Gakell, a cordwainer, was granted permission to erect a shop 'in a pillar on the north side of Elvet Bridge'.

By the middle of the eighteenth century, like Framwellgate Bridge, Elvet Bridge was burdened by chaotic over-development of, in the main, timber-framed buildings, constricting and overhanging the narrow carriageway and hampering the increasing traffic trying to cross. However picturesque and quaint this organic medieval growth might seem to modern eyes, to the eighteenth century men of influence in Durham it was unacceptable. Pressure came for clearance and in 1760 Henry Gakell's shop and others were removed. Forced removal of these makeshift structures was sometimes unnecessary – when a trader opened the door of his shop one morning in 1768 the floor fell into the river, shortly followed by the rest of the building.

The bridge was further changed following the Great Flood of 1771 when the three central arches were destroyed, again necessitating rebuilding. By the end of the eighteenth century the Paving Commissioners had formalised the clearances (p.128) and the situation was ripe for the bridge to be doubled in width in 1804-5 on the north side, covering in the old vennel on the peninsula. The work was designed and supervised by the County Bridge Surveyor, Christopher Ebdon.

Elvet Bridge, as we see it today, is a clean and sanitised structure where it crosses the river, but fortunately retains the enveloping buildings on both riverbanks. At the west end two concealed arches, probably the two leased to the chaplain of St James, were later converted to cells in the seventeenth century House of Correction. Adjoining these arches on the south side is an early nineteenth-century building (20 Elvet Bridge) whose lower basement incorporates medieval windows and a fine later arched doorway in its thick stonework and may represent the undercroft of the unidentified St James' Chapel.

At the east end, the remains of St Andrew's Chapel and chaplain's house survive on the rear wall of the bridge buildings – thin pilasters with the remains of three window openings between them (**37**). But these are contemporary with the arch beneath, which appears to be of original twelfth-century construction, suggesting that this widened section of the bridge may have accommodated a chapel from the beginning. If the bridge did indeed have fourteen arches, only ten are now identifiable. The western abutment is known, so the remaining four arches may lie on the east side beneath the road down to the junction with Old Elvet.

Only the briefest mention need be made of the little-known late medieval Bow Bridge that linked Elvet with the Bailey via Bow Lane. It would have been of particular value to the priory, enabling easier access to their eastern boroughs, although its construction would have compromised the military effectiveness of the river as a moat.

The bridges were good financial investments, bringing a steady income from rents and tolls. The priory contributed regularly towards maintenance costs, as did the bishop on occasions, through pavage grants raised from a tax on his tenants. Major rebuilding, however, was the bishop's sole responsibility. These funds were supplemented by income from the 'Briglands' – land and property donated by philanthropic citizens over the centuries for the maintenance and repair of Framwellgate, Elvet and Shincliffe Bridges.

37 *Elvet Bridge at its south-eastern end, with the broad section supporting the medieval chapel of St Andrew, whose lower walls are incorporated into later buildings.* City of Durham Council

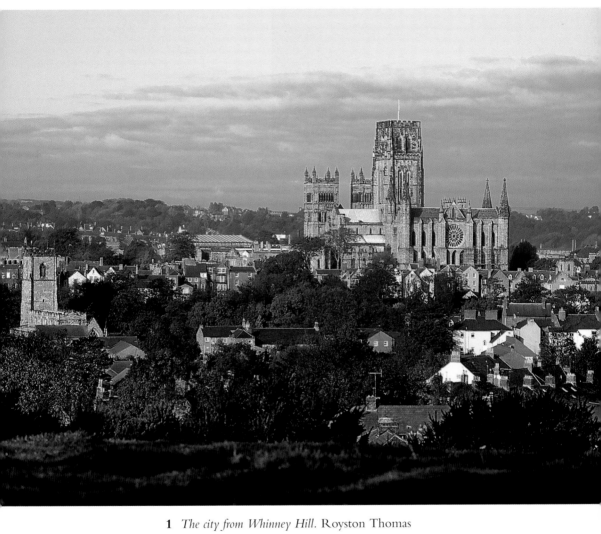

1 *The city from Whinney Hill.* Royston Thomas

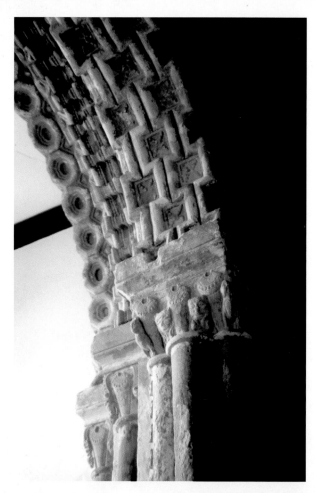

2 *(left) Le Puiset's doorway in the castle.* Martin Roberts

3 *(below) Aerial view of the city from the south-east.* Steve France

4 *(opposite) The Norman chapel in the castle.* Jarrold

5 *The castle keep.* Martin Roberts

6 *The great hall of the castle.* Royston Thomas

7 *The cathedral nave.* Royston Thomas

8 *The south-west tower of the cathedral.* Martin Roberts

9 *(right) The Galilee chapel in the cathedral.*
Royston Thomas

10 *(below) The priory refectory, now Dean*
Sudbury's Library, from the cloisters.
Martin Roberts

11 *(overleaf) The Chapel of the Nine Altars*
in the cathedral. Royston Thomas

12 *The priory kitchen from the College.* Martin Roberts

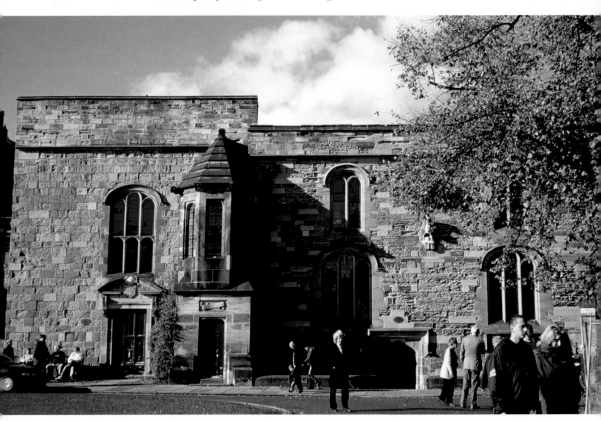

13 *Bishop Cosin's Library and the Exchequer, Palace Green.* Martin Roberts

14 *St Giles' Church from the south-east.* Martin Roberts

15 *St Oswald's Church interior.* Royston Thomas

16 *Neptune and St Nicholas' Church in the Market Place.* Royston Thomas

17 *Eighteenth-century Rococo plasterwork at Aykley Heads.* City Council

18 *Door cases in Old Elvet.* Royston Thomas

19 *Elvet Bridge: a 'Paving Commissioners' corner.* Martin Roberts

20 *Bishop Cosin's Hall and Almshouses, Palace Green.* Royston Thomas

21 *Prebends Bridge.* Royston Thomas

22 *'The Upper Room' sculpture by Colin Wilbourn.* Royston Thomas

23 *St Mary-the-Less Church, South Bailey.* Royston Thomas

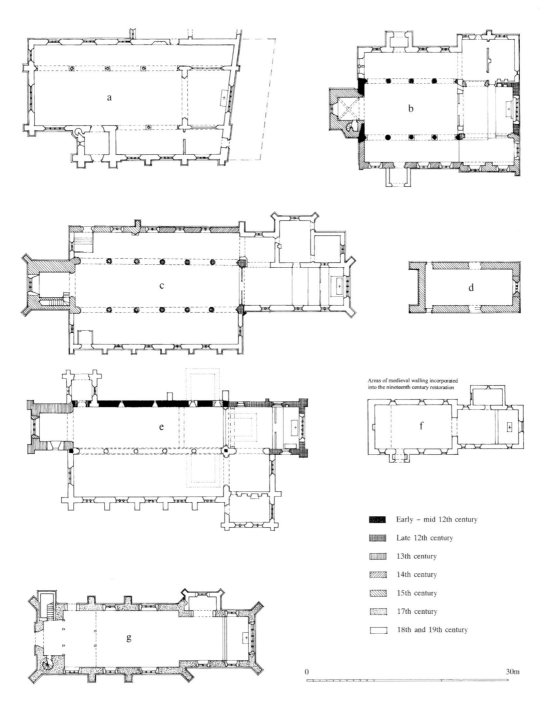

Areas of medieval walling incorporated
into the nineteenth century restoration

Early – mid 12th century

Late 12th century

13th century

14th century

15th century

17th century

18th and 19th century

0   30m

38 *The medieval churches and chapels: (a) St Nicholas (b) St Margaret (c) St Oswald (d) St Mary Magdalene (e) St Giles (f) St Mary-the-Less (g) St Mary-le-Bow*

Churches

Each of the boroughs of Durham had its own church except the Elvet Borough that used St Oswald's in the adjacent Barony of Elvet (**38**).

St Oswald's Church, the oldest and grandest, was perhaps always predominant among them. It may have originated in a pre-Cuthbertine settlement. No physical remains have yet been found but documentary evidence and the appearance of a circular churchyard on early maps have been cited in support of the claim. An Anglo-Saxon cross shaft and roof finial of late tenth- or early eleventh-century date, found reused in church walls, is further evidence. St Oswald's had a large parish that embraced the Old Borough, including its chapel of St Margaret of Antioch in Crossgate. This borough was fiercely independent and fought to establish marriages and burials in its own church, both finally allowed by the priory in 1431. It did not achieve separate parish status until the nineteenth century. The first church, probably founded around 1150, consisted of a nave with clerestory, south aisle, chancel and possibly a small western tower. The south aisle remains: squat piers with scalloped capitals and low round arches.

The north aisle of St Margaret was added (*c.*1195) and its arcade is a great contrast to the earlier work. It resembles the major building at St Oswald's of the same date, of which the chancel arch and four eastern bays of the nave survive. These late Norman arcades have a little of the elegance of the Gothic style to come, yet still retain plain circular Norman piers and round-headed arches (**colour plate 15**). They seem to represent building campaigns that are both a delayed restoration of churches damaged in Cumin's usurpation of the bishopric (1143-4) and an enlargement to accommodate the town's rapidly growing population. It must have been a generous enlargement for there is little evidence of any major church work in Durham during the thirteenth century when the town was still developing. This does not, of course, take account of the church of St Nicholas in the Market Place, first mentioned around 1133-41, whose medieval development is unknown as the present church is wholly Victorian. It is believed to have had a twelfth-century north chancel aisle and much of the rest of the church was thought to be late medieval (**39**).

St Giles' Church was founded as part of Bishop Flambard's hospital (*c.*1112) and from that period remains the impressively austere north wall, with three widely-spaced small windows high up. The original chapel may have been cruciform in plan, with small transepts and a crossing or central tower. An alternative suggestion is that the central and western part of the nave of the present church was the main hall of the hospital and its eastern part was the chapel. Le Puiset later refounded the hospital at Kepier and restored the former chapel for the exclusive use of the borough. A new chancel was built in characteristic late Norman style (**colour plate 14**). The remains of the chancel arch still exist with a boldly modelled zigzag motif forming hoodmoulds to

39 *Old St Nicholas' Church, (c.1855). The much altered medieval church is shown here just prior to demolition, with its truncated east end of 1841, caused by the widening of Claypath at its point of entry into the Market Place*

two windows, shafted inside and out – inside with waterleaf capitals. A little later the lower stages of the west tower were built.

The four medieval borough churches were complemented by two smaller garrison churches within the castle walls: St Mary-le-Bow and St Mary-the-Less. The latter may have been a late twelfth-century building to judge from architectural fragments saved from the rebuilding of the church last century (**colour plate 23**). At the beginning of the fourteenth century, as part of the construction of the town walls around the Market Place, St Nicholas' north wall was greatly strengthened to form part of the defensive line – reflecting contemporary practice in the new walled towns of North Wales (Conwy, Caernarfon).

From the early years of the thirteenth century until the end of the medieval period, there is little in the way of church enlargement in Durham beyond aisle widening. St Oswald's north aisle and chancel were rebuilt in the fourteenth century and, in 1343, St Margaret's south aisle was reconstructed. Only the two westernmost bays of the nave of St Oswald's appear to be a significant expansion around 1412, at a time when the town's population was thought to be static if not declining. Could it have been a rebuilding of earlier work? At the same time the clerestory was constructed and the tower added. The upper stages of St Giles' tower followed in 1414 and St Margaret's received a tower, clerestory and chancel chapels in the same period, perhaps in an effort to gain parochial status.

Little further work was done on the churches in the later medieval period and the most significant event in the seventeenth century was the collapse in 1637 of St Mary-le-Bow, following the fall of the adjoining gate. Rebuilding began around 1671 and was completed fourteen years later. The tower, completed around 1702, incorporates the remains of the gate's stone newel stair. The glory of the church is its fine contemporary furnishings. The magnificent woodwork of St Mary-le-Bow dates from the late seventeenth century, but many of the city's churches may have followed the example of the cathedral by installing new furnishings earlier, in the 1620s and 1630s. Such items are recorded at St Oswald's in the early 1630s. These improvements were in response to a group of clerics known as the Arminians, well represented in Durham, who advocated an enrichment of church liturgy and furnishings, the so-called 'beauty of holiness', as a reaction to the Puritanism of the Elizabethan church (p.72).

The St Oswald furnishings were probably lost in the restorations of 1834, 1864 and 1883; those at St Mary-le-Bow fortunately survived the restorations of 1833 and 1873. Other city churches were not so lucky and many earlier features and fittings disappeared in the nineteenth-century restorations of St Margaret's (1865 and 1877-80) and St Giles' (1828 and 1873). St Mary-the-Less is said to be a complete rebuild in Norman style to the original nave and chancel plan (1847), but the evidence suggests that substantial portions of the north wall at the very least were retained. Nothing was kept of the medieval St Nicholas', first shortened in 1841, then totally rebuilt in 1857 to the designs of J.P. Pritchett. It was built to the original medieval plan and form, with the addition of a tall spire to its tower (**colour plate 16**). It is a fine church, still active in the daily life of the Market Place. Only St Mary-le-Bow has ceased as a place of worship, now Durham Heritage Centre, while St Mary-the-Less is St John's College chapel, now splendidly refurnished.

The churches of Durham appear by the late medieval period to be commodious and comfortable, but lack the ostentatious displays of wealth that so often indicate the beneficence of powerful local merchants or gentry. The evidence is not comprehensive; the town has lost the medieval St Nicholas'. But the general documentary evidence suggests a small-scale merchant class and the surviving architectural evidence reinforces the view that there was a significant lack of civic power that in many towns would have found expression in its churches.

Public buildings

Apart from the churches, the public buildings of the medieval town have almost entirely vanished. They fall into three groups: firstly, the accommodation necessary for the town's guilds, secondly the borough's administrative buildings, lastly the mills and bakehouses provided for each borough by the city's overlords – the bishop, the priory and Kepier Hospital. Unlike most medieval towns, because of the distinctive borough development in Durham, public buildings were evenly dispersed throughout the town and not concentrated in one place.

Guild buildings in Durham mean religious guilds. Significantly, craft guilds developed late and have left no evidence at all of occupying buildings of their own. The religious guildhalls or houses may be briefly summarised: St Nicholas' (Market Place), St Cuthbert's (Claypath) and St Margaret's (Framwellgate) are all mentioned in the late thirteenth century. 'Mawdeleyngyldhouse' in North Bailey was abandoned by 1427. Corpus Christi (Walkergate) and Holy Trinity (Old Elvet) are both referred to in fifteenth-century documents. St Nicholas was the only guild that occupied a guildhall rather than a guildhouse. It was converted from an imposing private stone house around 1271 and may have been the one secular public building of any size in the medieval town beyond the peninsula fortress. Like many other guildhalls or houses, it declined in the later medieval period.

The borough courthouses were built centrally in each borough as administrative as well as judicial centres. Here tenants paid their rents, and tolls and fines were collected. They were mostly purpose-built but, in the Barony of Elvet, the hall in the priory's estate farm at Elvethall in Hallgarth Street was used while, in Elvet Borough, the prior used the Holy Trinity guildhouse when required. The courthouse in the Bishop's Borough was called 'le Tollbooth' and was situated in the Market Place near Fleshergate. In the late fourteenth century it was described as a first floor room with stalls below, probably of timber construction.

The mills and bakehouses were erected in each borough by their overlords to enable their tenants to comply with their tenurial obligations to grind corn and bake bread only within their own borough. Although they were a stimulus to the local economy, their weirs were a check on the development of river-borne trade. At one time or another, there were eight mills in the town, six priory owned and one each belonging to the bishop and Kepier Hospital. They were usually corn mills, though two were once used for fulling cloth. Scaltok Mill, at the eastern extremity of Elvet Barony beside one of the Wear's meanders, was established in the twelfth century but abandoned by the priory in 1462 after the river changed course. Milling moved to the surviving South Street Mill which had two mill wheels (**40**). On the opposite bank was the priory's own mill, to which a second was later added around 1416. These were known as Lead Mill and Jesus Mill, both now absorbed within the present Fulling Mill Archaeological Museum. The Bishop's Mill, mentioned in the Boldon Book (*c.*1183), stood on the weir downstream from Framwellgate Bridge, opposite the priory's Clock Mill on the Milneburn.

40 *South Street mill and millhouse.* David Roberts

Bishop's Mill, like South Street and Lead/Jesus Mills, still stands with mill buildings on site, but they appear to be entirely post-medieval. The mill building at South Street, though much larger, appears to be of the same date (perhaps eighteenth-century), but perhaps built on earlier foundations. Those at the Archaeological Museum may incorporate medieval work but the mill at Kepier survives only as a site.

The evidence for bakehouses is purely documentary, but these must have been the focus in each borough for considerable social activity with almost daily visits by the womenfolk to bake their bread. Bakehouse Lane, on the boundary with Gilesgate, marks the site of the communal ovens in Gilesgate Borough. Those in the Bishop's Borough are referred to as early as the Boldon Book around 1183. The bakehouse in Elvet, near the bridge, had stone walls and a stone roof, whilst that in the Old Borough, also near its bridge, included accommodation of a solar, cellar and garden, presumably for the baker.

Hospitals

In common with most medieval towns, Durham had a number of religious institutions, established by the bishop or the priory, that provided help for the sick and elderly. Many of these hospitals also provided temporary lodgings for travellers and pilgrims. Kepier, at Gilesgate, was far and away the wealthiest in the county. The riverside hospital, refounded by Le Puiset around 1180, attracted many endowments including the relatively impoverished Borough of St Giles itself (**41**). The buildings included a chapel, an infirmary for the long-term care of the sick and a common dormitory and hall for the accommodation of pilgrims and travellers, all overseen by a master and thirteen brethren, six of whom were priests. The entire hospital was contained within a boundary wall that would have been entered through a gateway or gatehouse.

To support the hospital, the bishops of Durham granted land including the Norman villages of Clifton and Caldecotes to the north-east of the city, later to become the estate farms of Low and High Grange in modern Belmont. In 1545 the hospital was suppressed and became the home of a succession of lay owners, some of whom added significantly to the buildings on the site (chapter 5).

The full extent and content of the hospital at Kepier is hard to assess given the lack of archaeological research and the uncertainty of medieval hospital layouts which lacked the rigid discipline of monastic claustral buildings. The site of the chapel for example is unknown, though it probably lay on the south side of the courtyard close to the infirmary hall and dormitory. There is a very small sketch on Schwyzer's 1595 map of Durham suggesting a tower, either of the chapel, as at Sherburn Hospital, or perhaps a boundary fortification. Nevertheless what survives is of the greatest interest.

The principal building is the great fourteenth-century gatehouse providing the riverside entry into the hospital precinct. This heavily weathered building

41 *Kepier Hospital in the late eighteenth century. This view, by S.H. Grimm, from within the hospital courtyard, illustrates the medieval gatehouse and west range buildings of 1522 which still survive; the latter with its timber framing now cloaked in brick and stone.* British Library Add MS 15540 Number 21

bears the arms of Bishop Richard Bury and the Master of Kepier, Edmund Howard, which dates it to 1341-45. It may represent a rebuilding of an earlier gatehouse damaged either in the fire of 1306 or during Scottish raids (c.1311-15), in which Kepier is known to have suffered losses. Its vaulted central passage is flanked by rooms for the porter's lodge, with a central first floor room originally reached by a fine polygonal stair, similar to that of the deanery in the College. This was later abandoned in favour of a post-medieval flight of external steps.

Running north from the gatehouse is the long west range, now farm buildings. The main portion was originally timber-framed on the first floor and has retained a significant part of its framing and roof construction cocooned within later stone and brick walls. It has been tree-ring dated to 1522 and was probably a storage or service building for the hospital. A portion of the much later roof at the north end collapsed in 2001 and is awaiting repair. The farmhouse at Kepier is yet another important medieval survivor and its lower courses probably incorporate original late twelfth century stonework including an intriguing buried arch. Most of the upstanding building is of later medieval date with a large chimney stack and fine fifteenth-century windows. Its roof is also of fifteenth or sixteenth century date.

One of the greatest architectural losses in Durham in recent times was the demolition in 1964 of the great late medieval barn on the High Grange estate at Belmont. This was a huge building 154ft (47m) in length, far larger than any similar barn in the north-east of England and a powerful testament to the wealth of Kepier Hospital.

Elsewhere in Durham, the bishop established a leper hospital just north of the city at St Leonard's, near where St Cuthbert's church now stands, but nothing now remains. The priory, for its part, in the late thirteenth century provided for poor relatives of their monks in St Mary Magdalene Hospital in Gilesgate. In 1451, the chapel was rebuilt on a new site and, though ruined, still survives with its reused fourteenth-century east window (**38**). On the peninsula, the priory provided almshouses in the Bailey, with travellers and pilgrims catered for in their Maison Dieu in North Bailey. The bishop's Maison Dieu stood at the southern end of Silver Street.

Elvethall Manor

No account of the medieval town would be complete without reference to the priory's estate farm at Elvethall Manor in Hallgarth Street. To the fifteenth-century visitor viewing the city from the hills above Framwellgate, after the dominance of the peninsular buildings, the eye would be drawn next to the great barn roofs of the manor farm, rising above the surrounding cottages of Elvet. The farm was one of many priory estates and was adminis-

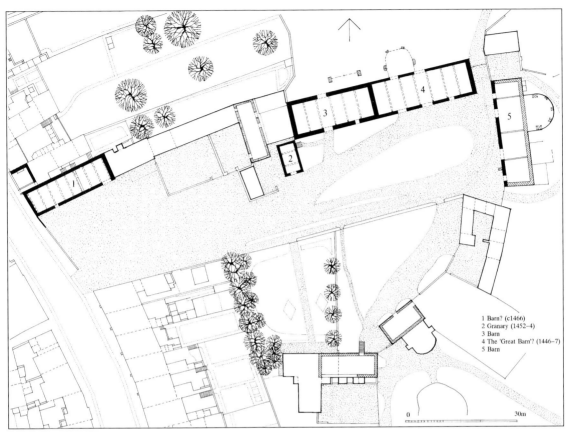

1 Barn? (c1466)
2 Granary (1452–4)
3 Barn
4 The 'Great Barn'? (1446–7)
5 Barn

0   30m

42 *Elvethall Manor in 1857, showing medieval buildings still surviving in the present day (shaded walls), probable medieval buildings since demolished (hatched) and probable post-medieval buildings since demolished (stippled and in thickened outline). The open farmyard onto Hallgarth Street was partially closed by the construction of numbers 21-32, c.1843 (bottom left). Four of the barns were adapted in the early nineteenth century by the addition of 'gin-gans', or horse engine houses. The priory farm is known today as the Hallgarth Tithebarns*

tered by their hostillar, the monk responsible for the priory guests and their accommodation. Its agricultural purpose was solely the production of corn. Part was retained for next year's seedcorn, part retained for internal consumption and part was for sale, barley being particularly convenient for the Elvet brewing trade.

The largest building was the 'Great Barn' with additional barns for wheat, barley and oats. There was a granary, byre, stables and stores. The reeve in charge lived in his own house on the farm, with additional houses for farm workers. Finally, the manor included a walled garden and a dovecote (**42**). The existing buildings now in use as Prison Offices and an Officers Club form one of the most remarkable medieval survivals in the town, despite alterations and adaptations. They have no known parallels in the north-east of England.

Six medieval buildings stand on the site, wholly or in part. More may await discovery. The major group is the two barns that lie in tandem, modernised last century. To the west lies the smaller and earlier barn with its tapering stone walls and great aisled truss roof structure. Parallels in Yorkshire suggest a date in the second half of the fourteenth century (**43**). Adjoining it is the largest barn on the farm, which may be identified with the 'Great Barn' possibly built in 1446-7. Both barns now have pantiled roofs but would originally have been stone-slated. At right angles to these barns, forming a corner of the great estate farmyard, is the wall of yet another barn which historical accident placed within the boundary of Durham Prison. The building was subsequently largely demolished, retaining its west wall as the prison's boundary wall (a status also shared by the 'Great Barn') until the construction of the new prison wall to the east.

Adjacent to the earliest barn is a rare building type – a medieval granary. The lower stone-walled cart shed supports the timber-framed grain store above. Documentary and tree-ring dating confirm a date of 1452-54. The priory accounts for the hostillar of 1452-53 record in detail the building of its walls by John Knaith and William Usworth, the carpentry by Richard Halme, with the plasterwork executed the following year, after the plaster had been carted from Northallerton. The position of the granary is worthy of note – at

43 *Elvethall Manor. The interior of the westernmost of the central pair of barns in the farmyard, photographed c.1920. This barn has now been adapted for use as a Prison Officers Club. The medieval roof structure has no known parallels in the city.* Durham University Library: Edis Photographic Collection H34

right angles to the barn, projecting forward into the body of the farmyard. It was a location of some prominence, almost an obstruction to the working of the farm. This was perhaps deliberate and a measure of the building's status, recalling the similar central village locations afforded to the *horrea* of northern Spain. The granary held the seedcorn for the following year's sowing – it was the future investment that needed protecting from dampness, vermin and theft. It needed constant surveillance.

Much closer to Hallgarth Street lies the last substantial medieval farm building that has been identified – a stone structure of uncertain use but certain date. Its roof trusses have been tree-ring dated to around 1466. On the opposite, southern side of the farmyard stands the former farmhouse, rebuilt in the early years of the last century. This work included the reconstruction of an ancient building, used latterly as a granary, which abutted the farmhouse on its eastern side A number of its stout oak timbers were reused as floor joists in the new granary building.

Domestic buildings

The buildings described so far were the landmarks of the medieval town, set within the general mass of domestic buildings. What were these houses like? The physical evidence in the town is slight and this has led to the persuasive conclusion that Durham was a town whose urban architecture never asserted itself in a particularly permanent form, in marked contrast to the architecture of its overlords on the peninsula. Recent discoveries of high quality buildings do, however, qualify that assertion.

The tenement plots were the chief determinants of the house plan. In Durham they seem to have been established in their present form as early as the late eleventh century and remarkably still survive, long and narrow, end on to the street. There were variations in tenement size throughout the city and it was in the Bishop's Borough, in the streets around the Market Place, that the greatest commercial pressure resulted in the narrowest frontages and irregular plots on corners (**44**). In the outer boroughs, tenements were more regularly spaced and generous in size, as the pressure on land diminished. By the fifteenth and sixteenth centuries, in a time of prolonged recession in Durham, plots on the outer edges of the town were abandoned and reverted to closes and orchards.

This range of development pressure also found expression in the height of buildings. The narrow frontage houses of late medieval Durham, in Saddler and Silver Streets, were at least three storeys high, contrasting with the modest two storeys in streets in the outer boroughs. There is both physical and documentary evidence that single storey dwellings were common in areas such as Hallgarth Street, on the fringe of the town. Access along these narrow tenements was

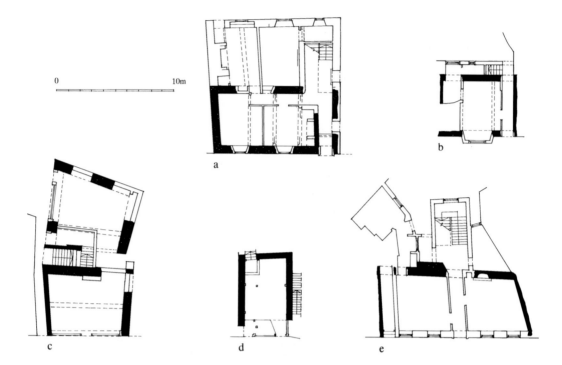

0   10m

a

b

c   d   e

44 *Medieval Houses; ground floor plans. (a) 22 Allergate: a late medieval front block, extended with a seventeenth-century kitchen wing and late eighteenth-century staircase. (b) 7 Crossgate: a small house with an eighteenth-century rear staircase extension. (c) 80 Saddler Street: two houses linked in the late seventeenth century by a staircase, constructed in the common vennel (after Clack). (d) 11 Silver Street: a small, but high-quality building, with internal passage and external vennel (now demolished). (e) 4 Church Street: foundations and rear stack survive from the early house plan, rebuilt with a new stair wing c.1700*

gained by alleys, called vennels in Durham. During much of the earlier medieval period, these vennels divided detached or semi-detached buildings and may have offered rudimentary protection against the spread of fire. However, as the pressure for development in the centre increased, by the fifteenth century they were built over to create continuous frontages. Modern developments and the gradual enclosure and 'privatisation' of vennels have greatly reduced their numbers, but the area behind Silver Street and Saddler Street still retains its original labyrinthine layout largely intact. The vennels also enabled separate dwellings to be built at the back of the long plots where expansion was possible, but the town's overlords penalised tenants for building them.

There were few stone houses of any importance in medieval Durham and these would be concentrated in the Baileys where the gentry and officials lived, and around the Market Place, the merchant quarter. Amongst the latter, Reginald Mercator's 'great hall of stone' would have been an outstanding landmark in the late thirteenth–century Market Place. Documentary references

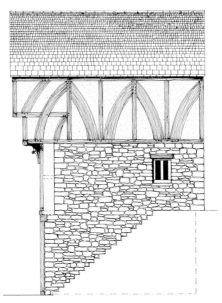

45 *11 Silver Street. A reconstruction of the side elevation of this early fifteenth-century building, based on the surviving evidence. The probability of a double jetty on the second floor façade is an unusual feature*

46 *22 Allergate. A reconstruction as built in the fifteenth or early sixteenth century, and its present appearance. The timber-framed construction was substantial, though lacking in the architectural details of the Silver Street house*

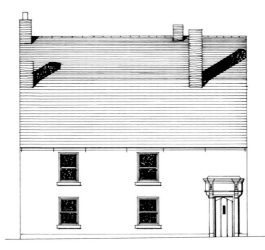

to stone houses may often disguise the use of timber framing for substantial parts of the upper storeys, and the evidence of the few buildings that do survive point to the use of stone for foundations, ground and occasionally first floor construction in largely timber-framed houses.

Late medieval houses in Owengate, Milburngate, Crossgate and Allergate retain stone ground floor walls, and the remarkable survival of a single side wall of an early fifteenth-century town house in Silver Street has stonework at first floor level too, doubtless to restrain the mound of the castle rising behind (**45**). This fine three-storey building does present the most recent evidence that the timber-framed buildings, at least in the Bishop's Borough, were of high quality with moulded beams and carved jetty brackets.

Jettying, the projection of upper storeys beyond the storey below by over-sailing timbers, appears primarily in the central areas of boroughs, used not only to maximise space but to suggest status. On the fringes of the late medieval town the unjettied 22 Allergate has particularly good framing surviving at the first floor level, with its original roof timbers intact; access at ground floor appears to be via a cross-passage behind a later stone fireplace (**46**). The timber-framed walls of this late medieval period are generally composed of full height posts in a frame often restrained at the corners with

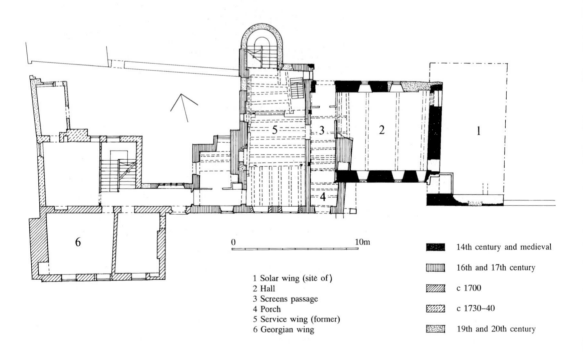

1 Solar wing (site of)
2 Hall
3 Screens passage
4 Porch
5 Service wing (former)
6 Georgian wing

0 _____ 10m

■ 14th century and medieval
▥ 16th and 17th century
▨ c 1700
▩ c 1730–40
▧ 19th and 20th century

47 *Crook Hall. The straggling and complex plan of the manor house illustrates the development of English domestic architecture over four centuries. Moving westwards, away from the old medieval hall, adaptations and additions of the seventeenth and eighteenth centuries provided more private and commodious apartments that led to the abandonment of the original building*

48 *The north wall of the medieval hall with the screens passage doorway and one of its ogee-headed lancets.* City of Durham Council

substantial curved bracing e.g. 11 Silver Street and 7 Crossgate. Small window openings, roughly framed by oak studs, still survive at 22 Allergate, 11 Silver Street and 83 Claypath.

Alongside these more durable timber buildings, there is documentary evidence to suggest that parts of the city were occupied by simpler tenements. These consisted of wattle-work houses of daubed panels supported on intermittent stakes – the cheapest construction for the poorer inhabitants. The predominant roofing materials for the medieval houses of the city would have been thatch (straw and heather) with stone slates for the better houses coming from nearby quarries in South Street. Their roof structures can still be found in a few houses in the town. One roof truss design in particular may have been common amongst late medieval houses of relatively modest status, and appears in 22 Allergate, 83 Claypath, 70 and 72 Hallgarth Street.

In complete contrast to the tightly-knit city centre streets, the countryside just beyond the urban edges of the medieval town supported a number of small estates, each centred on its manor house. The sole survivor is Crook Hall, a little to the north-east of Framwellgate and Sidegate. This 'precious medieval relic' as Pevsner described it, retains a fourteenth-century stone hall with an adjoining service cross-wing (**47**). Only the vestiges remain of the solar cross-wing at the opposite end of the hall, though evidence of its garderobe survives. The hall itself, recently beautifully restored, is lit by lancet windows of archaic form, albeit with fashionable ogee-arched heads. These appear to be of early fourteenth-century date, which may also be the date of a long deep ditch running beside the Hall's northern boundary – possibly an unfinished moat. The roof of the hall is later, constructed with truncated principal trusses around 1467-8. The service wing has stone walls on the ground floor, but its ceiling beams suggest that it was of jettied timber-framed construction on its upper floor. In the seventeenth and eighteenth centuries, a further wing and a fine Georgian town house of two periods were added to complete the ensemble (**48**).

The residents of the medieval town of Durham largely owed their livelihood to their overlords – principally the bishop and the priory – and were occupied in providing them with professional and clerical services, trades and craft skills as well as basic supplies. Within the town, life revolved round the market and the surrounding streets where the leather, textile and victualling trades congregated to serve their masters and the pilgrims who passed through the town. Yet these overlords, who gave the town its purpose, also denied it any real independence. They offered to its inhabitants no participation in local government and consequently no influential merchant class or craft guilds developed.

Despite the seemingly unhealthy situation, the townspeople never seemed to have rebelled against this authority. Their overlords were also their customers and employers and, though often conservative and slow to react, were not cruel or unjust. This arrested development was paid for in the appearance of the town. As Margaret Bonney has concluded:

> A visitor to Durham in the later middle ages would be left with the strong visual impression of the might of the church and the dominance of lordship in the town. Beneath the symbols of power on the peninsula lay a subservient urban community which lacked any powerful symbols of its own.

5

DURHAM 1550–1860

Late medieval Durham was dominated by its religious overlords, the bishop and the priory. After the Reformation, the bishop's power in particular experienced marked fluctuations – erosion, abolition, restoration and a final, unremitting decline – so that the 'prince-bishop' of 1536 had, by 1836, lost all his temporal authority. Over the same period the city had changed too, from a centre of political power to a provincial and moderately prosperous market town. Its role as a defensive bulwark against the turbulent Scots was finally extinguished after the Civil War and it developed more sedately as one of the United Kingdom's new 'Middle Shires'.

Sixteenth-century Durham, like many towns nationally, was in decline, a process noted in priory rents even before the dramatic events of the Dissolution. The decline was aggravated by the city's isolation from the centres of power as the bishop's authority waned. The great gentry families of the county, weakened by the Pilgrimage of Grace (1536) and the Rising of the North (1569) were in no position to build. There were no great monastic estates to exploit, convert or quarry for stone. But if the old nobility did not build, then a new social elite of cathedral clergy, professional men, wealthy tradesmen and the new coal owners increasingly took their place in the city. This new gentry focussed its building activity mainly on the peninsula where there was significant rebuilding and improvement of the Bailey houses in the late sixteenth century and particularly in the early part of the following century.

Much of this domestic rebuilding would have been of timber-framed construction, though stone would continue to be used for the most prestigious buildings. The vast majority of the city's timber-framed houses were replaced in brick in the late seventeenth and eighteenth centuries. This absence of physical evidence for the general maintenance and improvement of the city's buildings between the Reformation and Restoration has tended to support the view that little was built in this period. Current research has helped to remedy this imbalance. The Restoration did trigger a major rebuilding of the city in more permanent materials, but it should not obscure the evidence in documents (if less obviously on the ground) of the continued rebuilding of the city's medieval housing throughout the late sixteenth and early seventeenth centuries.

Nor should it be assumed that little or nothing was built during the troubled times of the Civil War and the Interregnum. During the relative peace after the Civil War, church repairs did not cease (St Oswald's) and there is both physical and documentary evidence of important building work in the wider region (Houghall, Croxdale and Bishop Auckland), even if the fabric is missing in the city itself.

The orthodoxy of excessive decay and spectacular revival, held by many historians in the last century, is receiving timely review. Bishop Cosin's own correspondence has, on occasions, served to promote this dramatic contrast, talking of 'rebuilding' when 'repair' is what actually took place. Nevertheless, in case the pendulum swings too far, the impact of his return and the post-1660 rebuilding still made an immense impact on a city twice occupied and damaged by the Scots in the preceding decades. The major reconstruction that took place after the Restoration swept away not only many of the domestic buildings of medieval Durham but also the evidence of post-Dissolution rebuilding. At the simplest level for example, we have a significant number of late seventeenth-century timber staircases in the city, yet not a single example from the first half of the century when we would expect any house of note to have one installed.

This rebuilding was generated not only by the need to improve, but also by the city's population growth during the late seventeenth and eighteenth centuries which, though not rapid, was accommodated largely within its medieval boundaries by extending existing buildings and allowing new back-plot development. All this had taken place without improvements in sanitation, and by the late eighteenth century the centre of Durham had become an unhealthy place to live. The narrow streets and alleys, densely packed within the obsolete medieval defences, were a breeding ground for disease and vermin.

The opening up of the city was brought about first by the decline in its military role. Later, it was encouraged by the influence of the eighteenth-century Paving Commissioners and their nineteenth-century successors, the Local Board of Health, empowered to seek improvements first in highways, then public health and sanitation. Cosin's destruction of the castle barbican in 1665 was one of the first manifestations, followed by the decision in 1685 not to rebuild the gate tower of St Mary-le-Bow across the Bailey. The Watergate was enlarged in 1778 for the new Prebends Bridge, and in 1791 the Clayport was demolished. The medieval bridges were doubled in width in 1804 (Elvet) and 1859 (Framwellgate) and, in 1820, after the last prisoners had transferred to the new gaol, the great North Gate was pulled down. Access to the Market Place was further improved by the truncation of St Nicholas' Church in 1841.

These changes created the opportunities for a gradual but sustained rebuilding of many of the city's public institutions and its private houses. Before considering them in detail, their context in the architectural development of the period should first be established.

Architectural development

Renaissance buildings

The Reformation in England coincided with the general introduction of Renaissance architecture from continental Europe. It arrived first through the court of Henry VIII and its adoption throughout the country blossomed in the great rebuilding of the former monastic estates. Its use was at first in decorative details, often on funerary monuments, then in architectural features such as doorcases, porches or fireplaces, before its full integration into architectural design.

In Durham, Renaissance architecture arrived late and then only modestly, but from the first in an architectural form. The open classical arcade, or loggia, was a hallmark of the new style and two, and possibly three, were built in the late sixteenth and early seventeenth centuries in the city (**49**). At Kepier Hospital, the Heaths laid out a new garden in the late sixteenth century, probably after 1588, and built centrally within it a new banqueting house of plain brick but with a three bay stone loggia looking south across the garden (chapter 7). The house is gone, but the arcade survives. In 1588 the County Court was rebuilt on Palace Green. It was rebuilt again in 1664 by Cosin, but the loggia of semi-circular arches along its front, shown in later engravings, may have been retained from the earlier building. The third example was built in the Market Place in 1617, where the old cross was surrounded by a square, twelve-arched loggia that stood until 1780. There was little else of architectural quality that has survived the rebuilding of later centuries.

The Cosin style: craftsmen and influences

The matter of John Cosin, prebend and Bishop of Durham, and the works he commissioned in the castle and cathedral has been discussed in earlier chapters. Some general comments are needed here on the status of his work, his architectural style and more detailed consideration of his woodwork. His influence in Durham covers two periods. The first was when he was a prebend of the cathedral (1624-1643) after which he fled to the continent where he spent the years of the Civil War and the Interregnum. The second period of residence followed his triumphant return to Durham as bishop (1660-72).

His architectural works in Durham are exclusively those he commissioned as bishop. It should be stressed that he was never the designer of any of his commissions but he nevertheless exerted a powerful influence over his projects and the craftsmen in his pay. His architecture tends to be conservative and, in its general use of quasi-Gothic and Tudor windows and doors, suggests the survival of the Gothic tradition but little more. His architectural 'style' can be hard to pin down. He seems not to be bound by any powerful orthodoxy and his decisions to employ sometimes classical and sometimes Tudor Gothic motifs cannot be rationally explained. As we have seen, he is respectful of

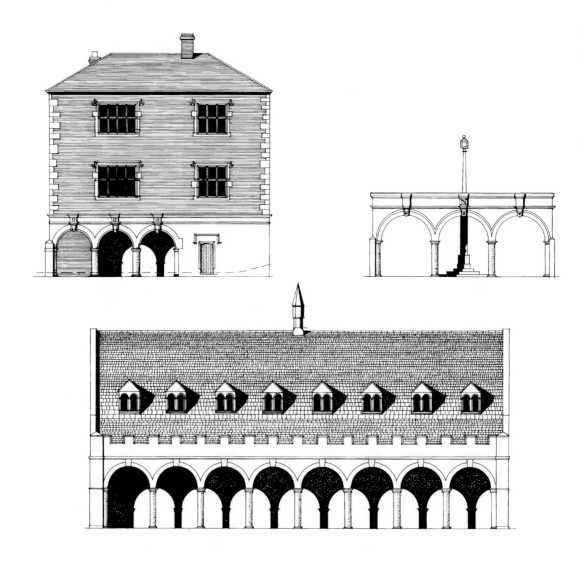

49 *Renaissance loggias. Kepier Hospital (above left) built after 1588, where the loggia was an innovative feature in an otherwise conservative banqueting house. The Old Market Cross of 1617 (above right) had very similar detailing to Kepier. The impressive County Court of 1588 substantially rebuilt in 1664, (below) is one of the city's major architectural losses. This suggested reconstruction is based upon a handful of minor, often conflicting, illustrations*

Tunstall's staircase in the castle, reflecting its Tudor design in the Black Stairs opposite, but he is content to accept a classical design for his Hall porch. His library door is also classical yet, when offered a similarly styled doorcase on his Almshouses on the opposite side of Palace Green, he chooses the more respectful Tudor design that we see today. The Almshouses were designed by his chief mason, in effect his architect, John Langstaffe, a Bishop Auckland Quaker employed extensively by Cosin (colour plate 20).

In these varying designs, Cosin is perhaps reflecting that freedom of design, based partially on conservatism and a lack of architectural dogma, that he knew from his days as Master of Peterhouse, Cambridge. In the early seventeenth century, away from royal court circles, both Oxford and Cambridge built their colleges in a broad palette of architectural styles, sometimes combining Gothic, classical and baroque themes in a single building. Nearer home, in Newcastle upon Tyne later in the century, the architect Robert Trollope was designing in the same stylistic mix in an equally exciting, if more bizarre, fashion, as in the town's Guildhall.

If the architecture of John Cosin remained relatively conservative, the woodwork that he commissioned and influenced throughout the county is far more spirited and robust. It covers both pre- and post-Civil War and Interregnum periods, and was predominantly church work, although the circle of craftsmen that he commissioned was able to execute secular work both for the bishop and others in the city and county. His early seventeenth-century commissions have their roots in the Arminian reforms of the 1620s and 1630s, instigated in the cathedral at Durham and spreading throughout the diocese. This work was often of very high quality, combining Gothic and Jacobean motifs (pp.72 & 100).

After the Interregnum, Cosin's return as bishop in 1660 prompts major restoration work in the cathedral and his two palaces at Auckland and Durham Castles (see respective chapters). The completion of his work at Auckland was influential, reflected in refurnishings in parish churches throughout the county. His Durham city work is of the finest provincial quality and exhibits the earlier mixture of styles but now combining the Gothic motifs with the fleshier sculptural qualities of the baroque, particularly strongly influenced by continental designs, most probably from the Netherlands or Germany. The Gothic designs here are not the reflex instincts of a dying style, rather there is a conscious revival of a whole range of medieval ornament – Norman zigzag and later nailhead for example. By employing the inherently rich decorative traditions of both the Gothic and baroque with the same exuberance, he demonstrated that they are not incompatible bedfellows (27).

Who were the craftsmen who executed this woodwork and what were their influences? The early seventeenth-century joiners and carpenters of the destroyed cathedral woodwork are unknown to us and one can only speculate whether Robert Barker, the carver of the Brancepeth and Sedgefield church-work, was employed in the city too. From the period after the Restoration (1660-72) we have a group of Durham city woodworkers identified in contracts, working between Bishop Auckland and Durham on the bishop's palace commissions, principally John Brasse, Abraham Smyth, James Hull and Marke Todd. James Hull (c.1633 to post-1698) often worked as a team with Todd and was employed by the bishop on most of his Durham buildings. Abraham Smyth not only worked on the bishop's prestigious commission but, as most carpenters and joiners would have done, also undertook important work for the local parish churches. Mention should also be made of the enigmatic James Clement, said to have been the carver of the cathedral choir stalls in 1660, author of no other known work and possibly the same man buried at St Oswald's in 1690 with the profession of 'architect'.

These were local men, mostly locally born and apprenticed. How did they achieve the skills and the knowledge of continental designs? The influence of continental books and prints was strong at the time, although the bishop appears to have had none in his extensive library. If the craftsmen themselves had no printed sources, they did have in Newcastle the notable school of early seventeenth-century woodwork in the city mansions and public buildings to study at first hand. Here were continental designs executed by an unknown woodworker of national status, displaying an exceptional talent in his work that incorporated Flemish influences, some of which reappear in the Cosin woodwork thirty years later in a less refined and more robust manner.

The greatest influence on these native woodworkers may have been Cosin's introduction of Dutch craftsmen for particular work. Hendrik de Keyser was a stone sculptor, while Jan Baptist van Eersell was a painter and 'lymner' of the woodwork. Others may have been in the bishop's pay – the artist V. Bok may have been one such (6). The influences may be complex but the collective body of work by these men and their rural counterparts, under the slightly misleading genus of 'Cosin woodwork', has been described by Pevsner as 'one of the most remarkable contributions of the county to the history of architecture and decoration in England'.

One of the first buildings in Durham to show baroque influence was, paradoxically, the remodelled medieval refectory, a conversion completed after 1684 into Dean Sudbury's library. Attempts at a wholly classical design, evident in the cloister door and the original semi-circular arched window openings, were compromised by the insertion of Gothic tracery in the window heads, a hybrid removed by Salvin's full Perpendicular Gothic restoration of the late 1850s.

The eighteenth and nineteenth centuries
The baroque of the early eighteenth century is best represented by 3 South Bailey (Haughton House), formerly the Eden family's town house, and the finest house in the Bailey with its imposing façade and strongly modelled stonework (50). It represents a rarity in Durham – a domestic property built

50 *3 South Bailey (Haughton House, St John's College) has the finest baroque façade on the peninsula, set back from the street to give it more presence.* Graeme Stearman

from scratch with a formal architectural façade. By the mid-eighteenth century the Palladian reaction to the baroque excesses had set in. In Durham a number of private houses are modestly representative of this change, such as 24 North Bailey and St Godric's Court (the former Castle Chare Arts Centre), both around 1760. Only the remodelling of the Guildhall in the Market Place in 1754 seems from engravings to have been a more substantial Palladian composition.

The little Conduit House in the College, erected the previous year, was the first building in Durham in the new Gothic Revival style. It may have been designed by Sanderson Miller, who most certainly was the architect for the remodelled rooms in the castle in 1753. He had been brought in by Bishop Butler who sought Miller's advice on obtaining craftsmen to execute the work because 'our people at Durham do not much understand the kind of Antique work'. Gothic Revival was part of the pluralism in design popular in the mid-eighteenth century. Durham has a fine collection of Rococo plasterwork interiors and even a hint in one or two of its staircases of the Chinese influence fashionable in furniture and garden follies. However, in a town with such major medieval monuments, it was perhaps inevitable that the Gothic Revival was most enduring in architectural design.

Wyatt's work at the end of the eighteenth century on both castle and cathedral was followed by Atkinson's castellated houses in the College (c.1808). Later still, the style was employed with more archaeological correctness by that most versatile of local architects, Ignatius Bonomi (1787-1870). Ignatius was the son of Guissepi Bonomi, an Italian architect who worked for Robert Adam in London. In 1813 he settled in Durham, having secured the job of County Bridge Surveyor; he developed a wide ranging architectural practice throughout the north-east, embracing county seats and workers' cottages, churches, prisons, courts, hospitals, bridges and restoration work on the cathedral. He involved himself fully in the life of the city and championed many improvements in social welfare, public health and education.

Like many of his contemporaries, notably John Dobson of Newcastle upon Tyne, he was called upon to display great versatility in architectural design, employing the Classical Revival style in his public buildings such as the Crown Courts (1814-21), Perpendicular Gothic in St Cuthbert's Roman Catholic Church, Old Elvet (1827), and Romanesque in his Market Place proposals (1841). His scholarly restoration work in the cathedral is quite uncharacteristic of its time (1828-40) and his enthusiasm for experimentation led to the use of the French mansard roof on Burn Hall, just outside Durham (1821-34), probably his finest building.

Bonomi also designed in the fashionable Greek Revival style at Eggleston Hall, near Barnard Castle, but in Durham the style is best represented in the small garden folly called the Count's House of around 1820, a perfect Doric temple in miniature and possibly Bonomi's work. It is also evident in the doorcases and railings of several houses (Leazes Place, *c*.1840, Crossgate Workhouse, 1837). Throughout the middle years of the nineteenth century, the two strands of Classical and Gothic Revival continued, represented in Durham by Gilesgate Station and the Market Place rebuildings of the Town Hall and St Nicholas' Church.

Public buildings

At the end of the medieval period, the administration of the palatinate was concentrated within the boundaries of the peninsula, the bishop's castle, the priory, the exchequer, the mint and so on. Aside from the local borough courts, the major judicial buildings were there too, with wrongdoers led only a short distance to the nearby North Gate gaol. The focus of this medieval power, the palatinate's forum, was Palace Green. Three centuries later, this had all gone. The administrative centre for the city moved to the Market Place and new judicial and penal buildings were built in green field sites off the peninsula. Palace Green had to adapt to a new role as the centre of the young university.

The civic and administrative buildings in Durham present a complex history not easily disentangled (**51**). The administrative centre for the medieval Bishop's Borough was the Tollbooth, probably a free-standing timber-framed building at the southern end of the Market Place near the entrance to Fleshergate. When Bishop Tunstall rebuilt it in stone on the western side (*c*.1535) the old site was occupied by a marble sanctuary cross from Gilesgate. In turn, this cross, or a replacement, was encased in the twelve arched loggia of 1617, which served as a covered market as the old Tollbooth had done (**49**). This was removed in 1780 and a new arcaded 'piazza' was constructed against St Nicholas' churchyard, which survived until the construction of the new indoor market in 1852.

Into this cluttered forum came the lead figure of Neptune in 1729, erected on top of the stone wellhead, symbolising aspirations for Durham to be linked to the sea by making the Wear navigable (**colour plate 16**). It came to nothing. In 1861 he was joined by the imperious equestrian statue of the third Marquis of Londonderry, by the sculptor, Monti. Tunstall's new Tollbooth had, by the seventeenth century, become known as the Guildhall and stood on the site of the present Guildhall. Bishop Cosin is said to have rebuilt it in 1665 and much of the present structure must date from this period. In 1754, the building was greatly altered, notably its façade which received a fashionable classical design with a large central semi-circular window and roof top cupola (**52**). It was designed by John Bell, a Durham architect who worked at times as clerk of works for the more illustrious architect James Paine. Two years earlier the Old Town Hall, built to the rear of the Guildhall in the late seventeenth

51 *The pant or well head in the Market Place, looking towards Silver Street, c.1860. The statue of Neptune, first erected in 1729, was replaced on a second pant in 1863, and a third in 1902. Finally removed in 1923, Neptune languished in Wharton Park until his return in 1991.* Durham University Library: Gibby Collection

century, was raised and panelled, and in the nineteenth century it was doubled to its present size.

By the mid-nineteenth century, the increasing business of the City Council required a major enlargement of the civic buildings. The area between the Town Hall and St Nicholas' had, since the sixteenth century, been occupied by the palatial courtyard town house of the Earls of Westmorland, known as New Place. Their occupation was relatively brief, as the property was forfeited to the crown after the earl's participation in the ill-fated Rising of the North in 1569. These ancient buildings were cleared for the new Town Hall and Market (1848-52).

The architect for the new buildings was P.C. Hardwick who employed a Perpendicular Tudor style. The main addition was the new Town Hall itself, a large room with a superb hammerbeam roof that projects into and rises above the new market. The butter market was relocated beneath the arches of the new hall, maintaining the traditions of the medieval Tollbooth. At the same time, the Guildhall was renovated in a matching Gothic style but retaining the

52 *The remodelled Guildhall of 1754 with its Palladian façade designed by John Bell and beside it, New Place, an ancient jettied building, the former town house of the Earls of Westmorland (above) as they may have appeared prior to their redevelopment as the new Town Hall and Market of 1848-52 (below)*

eighteenth-century formality, substituting traceried Gothic for pedimented classical, fleche for cupola. The result is an approachable and unpretentious building that sits well in the Market Place.

The judicial and penal institutions in the city developed from the peninsula. The medieval assize court of the bishop was rebuilt in 1588 on the north side of Windy Gap passage on Palace Green. The sixteenth-century building was constructed of wood and, in 1664, it was rebuilt by Bishop Cosin and known as the County or Sessions House. John Langstaffe is said to have built it. Little more is known of it, but an undated memorandum from Bishop Cosin clearly refers to a two-storey building with eight or nine dormer windows rising 'from the cornish [cornice] after the Italian fashion'. If the classical loggia across its façade with its medieval crenellated parapet were Cosin's rather than a retention of part of the 1588 building, it demonstrates again his pluralist approach to design (**49**).

By the eighteenth century, consciences were aroused by the insanitary and inhumane conditions in which prisoners were kept in the North Gate gaol and, in 1809, a new County (now Crown) Court and Gaol were begun on open land at the far end of Old Elvet. The architect was Francis Sandys and the Assize Court was in use for a while in 1811. However, complaints about poor workmanship and delays led to Sandys' replacement the following year when George Moneypenny took charge. Some demolition of new work was needed and the prison was replanned. Moneypenny was replaced by Ignatius Bonomi in 1814 when the full extent of the building's defects became apparent. Inadequate foundations, rubble-filled walls and stone-faced wooden columns necessitated even more substantial demolition and rebuilding. From this costly and chaotic fiasco, Bonomi fashioned a handsome building and established his good name. The façade is constructed of the finest ashlarwork with Tuscan columns, between which four blocked putlog holes in the stonework identify the position of the demountable scaffold for public executions (**53**). Bonomi's County Court interior was lost in the unfortunate reordering around 1870 by W. Crozier – the cumbersome balustrading would have been more at home on the seafront at Whitley Bay.

Bonomi's work can also be seen in the large prison erected behind the Crown Courts. The first prisoners arrived in 1819 from North Gate gaol and the new buildings were completed in 1821. The gaol had three wings, male and female blocks and a debtors' prison. Bonomi remained in charge of prison buildings until 1850 and designed additions in 1825, 1828 and 1842, when a separation system to isolate hardened criminals necessitated further building work.

The population growth in the centuries after the Reformation was sufficiently modest that there was no need to undertake major Anglican church building. New work concentrated largely upon satisfying the needs of a growing non-conformist community in Durham. Presbyterians established a place of worship in 1672 in Claypath, replaced in 1750 by the brick chapel still

53 *The new Crown Courts, 1809-21, by Francis Sandys, George Moneypenny and Ignatius Bonomi.* David Roberts

standing, well-concealed, behind the later Reform Church. Congregationalists, established in Framwellgate in 1778, later joined with them. Three strains of Methodism developed in Durham. Wesleyans, established in 1743, converted a building into a chapel in Rotten Row in 1770 and built a new one in Old Elvet in 1808. The Primitive Methodist chapel, in use 1825-62, still survives as a shell behind 33 Silver Street while the New Connexion, after starting in Old Elvet in 1828, moved to their new Bethel Chapel in North Road in 1853. This sturdy building was designed by E.R. Robson in the classical chapel style and has a superb interior with a sweeping gallery of high pews, spoilt only by its modernised, if more welcoming, ground floor layout.

Quakers have long been associated with Claypath but their 1679 meeting house disappeared in the nineteenth century. Only a few forlorn graves in part of their burial ground survive. Old Elvet was likewise known as the centre of the Roman Catholic community. There were two chapels here in the late seventeenth century and in 1827 a new church, St Cuthbert's, was built to the design of Bonomi; it was well-proportioned Gothic externally, but thinner and more elegant within.

Developments in education, like so much in Durham, emanated from the peninsula. The small priory song school, reformed in 1430, still survives in the

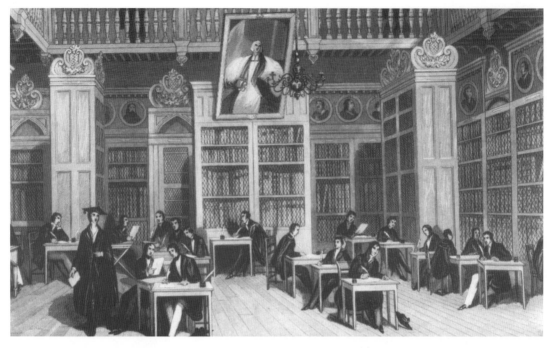

54 *Bishop Cosin's Library: a view of the interior in the mid-nineteenth century when the library was used for university examinations. The gallery was an addition of 1834.* Durham University Library

present Choristers School in the College. The Almoner's School, outside the priory gate, was probably in existence in the mid-fourteenth century and served as a preparatory school for entry into the monastic community. In 1414 Bishop Langley founded two schools for the teaching of music and grammar on the east side of Palace Green and these were refounded by Bishop Cosin in 1667-8 after their destruction by the Scots in 1640. His architect, John Langstaffe, balanced the schools like bookends at either end of the bishop's almshouses. The ensemble still stands, old-fashioned but pleasant, if emasculated by the loss of its chimneys.

In 1661 Cosin had also rebuilt the grammar school, refounded at the Reformation from the priory Almoner's School, on the south-west corner of Palace Green, with a typical Cosin Gothic window in its east gable. In 1844, it was re-established as Durham School in Quarryheads Lane. Bishop Cosin's munificence in the Restoration period found yet further expression in his library on Palace Green. He was, throughout his life, an active collector of books and during his exile more than 1,000 volumes were held by his old college at Peterhouse in Cambridge. Thus, in 1667-8, Cosin again sought the services of Langstaffe to design a building to house his collection that would be dedicated for public use (**54**). The library interior was almost a double cube and its wall shelving, with intermediate niches for readers, was an innovation influenced by Cosin's familiarity in exile with the *Bibliothèque Mazarine* in

Paris. Externally the façade demonstrates admirably the breadth and the enigma of Cosin's taste – both Gothic window and the baroque door below are part of the original design (**colour plate 13**). The building lost some of its elegance in a heavy nineteenth-century restoration when the balustraded parapet was lost.

The provision of educational facilities in Durham was not exclusively the domain of the established church. Sadly, those lesser private ventures of the eighteenth and nineteenth centuries have left little trace in standing buildings. Schools established by individual philanthropists and private enterprise were popular in the first half of the nineteenth century, but most closed; later foundations, the Bow School of 1885 and Durham High School for Girls (1884) survive to represent the tradition.

The Durham Mechanics Institute was established in 1825 to promote good practice amongst the trades of its members. Its educational objectives widened and embraced art, history and astronomy as well as attracting support from such worthies as the émigré French artist, Bouet, and the architect, Bonomi. A purpose-built Institute was finally erected in 1841 in Claypath to Bonomi's designs. It has an imposing if plain façade, behind which is a large first floor hall.

The major event in Durham's educational history is the foundation of the university in 1832. An attempt had been made in 1650 to establish a college in the former prebendal houses of the Dean and Chapter. Letters patent were issued seven years later and the college probably opened but, after an attempt to gain university status in 1658-9, it only survived until the Restoration a year later.

The University of Durham Act became law on 4 July 1832 and after a brief residency in the Archdeacon's Inn on Palace Green (now Bishop Cosin's Hall), the first college, University College, moved to Salvin's rebuilt keep in the castle in 1840. Salvin also designed new buildings at Hatfield College, which in 1846 became the university's second college. He was also employed to design the observatory (1840), a classical domed building of Greek cross plan. To facilitate astronomical observation, a north point was constructed in the form of an obelisk in 1850, on the estate of Alderman W.L. Wharton at Dryburn.

The Georgian theatres of eighteenth-century Durham contributed considerably to the cultural life of the city. The earliest, mentioned as new in 1722, probably stood on the north side of the steep vennel, Drury Lane, leading from Saddler Street to the Wear. It was rebuilt in 1771 with a small auditorium only 9 by 14.4m (30 by 48ft) but closed after 1785 following a legal dispute. The demand for a theatre remained and, although a second had opened in Hallgarth Street in 1760, a new Saddler Street theatre was built behind the Lord Nelson Inn (now the Shakespeare) in 1792. It was burnt down in 1869 and only its gable wall remains against the back of the public house. However, the vennel entry to the pub is a reminder of the shortest distance between the pit and the bar.

The best survival is the eighteenth-century Assembly Rooms, much altered in a nineteenth-century enlargement, but still in active use. This was the centre of entertainment in Durham where fashionable society gathered for concerts, balls etc. and retains fine eighteenth-century plasterwork as evidence of its former grandeur.

In 1785 a dispensary in Saddler Street was provided for the relief of the sick and proved so successful that an infirmary was established in Allergate seven years later. This was run by private subscription and closed in 1853 when the County Hospital was opened in the then rural setting at the top of North Road. Its large Jacobean façade is now unfortunately concealed by later additions. In 1837, after the Poor Law Amendment Act of three years earlier, the construction of the workhouse in Crossgate was complete. The original plain stone terrace was part of the former hospital of St Margaret's, now converted to a variety of new uses.

The coming of the railways to Durham began with the construction of a terminus at Gilesgate in 1844 for the Durham and Sunderland Railway. The station was designed by G.T. Andrews and is now a hotel behind its classical façade. There was also a station at the head of Old Elvet, where the Magistrates Court now stands. Fortunately the main station remains in use. It was built in 1857 for the North Eastern Railway Company and designed by T. Prosser. In the same year the company constructed the impressive eleven-arched viaduct to bridge Flass Vale and North Road.

The Durham Paving Commissioners

Brief mention has already been made in the introduction to this chapter of the role of the Paving Commissioners in the opening up of the city in the eighteenth century. Their influence on the appearance of the city merits further discussion. The first Durham Paving Act of 1773 established for the first time a central administration under a single surveyor for all pavements, sewers, drains, watercourses, footpaths, carriageways and lamps. This act was superseded by the more important Act of 1790, which, as far as paving was concerned, again failed to improve conditions. Only an amended Act of 1822 finally brought action and improvement.

The 1790 Act did, however, focus on the problems of constriction of the highway, noting that the streets 'are rendered very inconvenient by several nuisances, annoyances, encroachments and obstructions'. In an appendix to the original bill and amended in the final act, the commissioners listed specific properties that were obstructions to the highway and which, with their new powers, were to be purchased by them for resale and redevelopment on the original, or an improved, building line. Acquisitions began the following year. The properties targeted did not yet bear house numbers, but were identified in the act by street and then by their relationship to adjacent occupiers. This complicates the task of identification but corner properties can easily be spotted and the consequences of acquisition readily appreciated.

Up to the Restoration, the buildings on the street corners of Durham would, like most of the city, be of timber-framed construction of a square or rectangular plan. Like those buildings surviving in Silver Street and Owengate, they would have had projecting upper floors or jetties, extending out over the street (**45** & **52**). Corner buildings would be jettied on both street frontages and, in many cases, would have been buildings of some prestige with high quality woodwork displayed on their prominent façades.

The Paving Commissioners would see double benefit in corner properties. Not only could encroachments and overhanging storeys be removed but the street junction could be widened with a gently curving building line replacing the sharp corner of the old building. This has given Durham a familiar sight – two, three or four storey brick façades sweeping the street corner with neat rows of sashed windows under a slated roof. Similar buildings can be identified in the streets themselves, where a particularly troublesome property needed to be cleared away.

Achieving these improvements may have required the complete removal of the offending building and this was particularly the case with corner proper-ties, where remodelling two façades often destabilised the structure of the whole building. The prestigious 'Cornerbooth' building on the corner of the Market Place and Saddler Street has been entirely removed, the new building perhaps little more than half the size, on plan, of its predecessor. The corner of South Street and Framwellgate Bridge is now a rather sad bit of greenery but is redeemed by the end wall of a medieval timber-framed building left locked in a neighbouring property, shorn of its jetties. It was left in place when the rest of the building was removed for a curved Commissioners' building, whose memory survives in the boundary wall. Occasionally a corner building could be adapted and not demolished. The long building at the junction of Elvet Bridge and New Elvet retains its late medieval roof structure, albeit remodelled and truncated, behind its new curved façade (**colour plate 19**).

The Commissioners' work has undoubtedly robbed us of some of the city's more picturesque, and sometimes architecturally important, buildings. The case of 70 Saddler Street is relevant as it may well have been one of the Commissioners' targets. It was, and largely still is, a late medieval timber-framed and jettied building with a possible rear hall range beside the Saddler's Yard vennel. Its front range timberwork does lean towards the street and its original jettied front must have appeared to dip alarmingly in the eighteenth century. This movement may have been the result of distortion of the green timber soon after construction or it may have been evidence of the later decay. In any event the new brick façade that was erected gradually cut back the offending overhangs and presented a tidy appearance that prevented further movement.

The building materials used in these late eighteenth century and early nineteenth century improvements were invariably modest provincial Georgian brick and slate (probably Westmorland, not Welsh), and this theme was generally continued in the widening of the medieval bridges, many of whose bridgehead properties were on the Commissioners' list too.

The later removal of the North Gate and its barbican in 1820 created a large gap in Saddler Street, filled by buildings with a little more architectural quality, notably the fine stone façade of the Reading Room and Subscription Library on Owengate corner. When the House of Correction at the bottom of the peninsula side of Elvet Bridge was sold in 1821, new buildings arose above the old prison cells and workshops on both sides of the street. These were more fittingly designed to the newly widened highway and gave this part of the town a modest late Georgian character. Beside these municipal initiatives, the individual improvements in the city's buildings need considering next.

Domestic buildings

The greatest change in the appearance of Durham between 1550 and 1860 arose from the rebuilding of its houses. Timber-framing was gradually replaced by brick and stone, while the increasing population encouraged extension both upwards and backwards into burgage plots. The first 100 years of this period were ones of economic and political decline, only aggravated by the depredations of the Civil War. As noted at the beginning of this chapter, rebuilding did take place but the physical evidence has all too often been swept away in later improvements. Dating of fabric in this period is difficult without architectural features, so often later replaced. Still, the brick-infilled framing of 32 Silver Street is an example of the post-medieval timber-framed tradition that has survived.

The greatest redevelopment occurred between 1660-1760, particularly in the early years after the Restoration. It seems there is scarcely a building in the city that was not altered in some way during this period. It is difficult to appreciate how extensive this reconstruction must have been throughout the city, from cathedral to cottage, with streets encumbered by scaffolding and the constant sight of builders at work throughout the town. There was no better symbol of the confidence of this period than the displays of curved brick gables of the new houses on the peninsula. These were displayed not to the front of the street, where often earlier buildings survived, but to the rear, high up above the river, full of self-importance (55).

The period from the mid-eighteenth to mid-nineteenth century saw a continued, if less dramatic, scale of development with changes in fashion dictating improvements to the façades and the interiors of earlier buildings. The end of the period was marked by the emergence of formal terraces, the urban form that was to dominate the rest of the nineteenth century.

House plans

The houses of medieval Durham varied considerably, depending upon the width of their burgage plots, their position in the town and, of course, the social status of their occupiers (**56**). Wide frontages did not always indicate wealthier citizens. In the tightly built streets around the Market Place such frontages would be extremely rare and even moderately prosperous people, such as those who built 11 Silver Street in the fifteenth century, were confined to narrow plots. Conversely, on the edges of the outer boroughs in Allergate or Hallgarth Street, broader plots may have been occupied by much poorer members of the community. In the centre of the boroughs, house plans would have had to accommodate ground floor shops, and vennels or enclosed passages gave access to the rear and upper floors.

This then was the inheritance of post-Reformation Durham, and the innumerable changes, not only in house plans but also between adjacent burgage plots, reveal a great deal about the social structure of the town at particular periods. Rarely was a house rebuilt completely from scratch; more often than not the existing building was incorporated into the new work. Earlier cellars, stone ground floor walls and timber framed cross-walls are strong clues to such medieval survivals.

The simplest improvement to an existing house was usually the provision of a proper staircase. At 7 Crossgate, one was added against the rear wall of the timber-framed house and, at 80 Saddler Street, a fine late seventeenth-century staircase was constructed in an external yard, amalgamating two jettied timber

55 *The rear elevations of (from left to right) 40-38 Saddler Street and 8 Saddler Street, as they may have appeared at the end of the seventeenth century, showing the fine displays of curved brick gables*

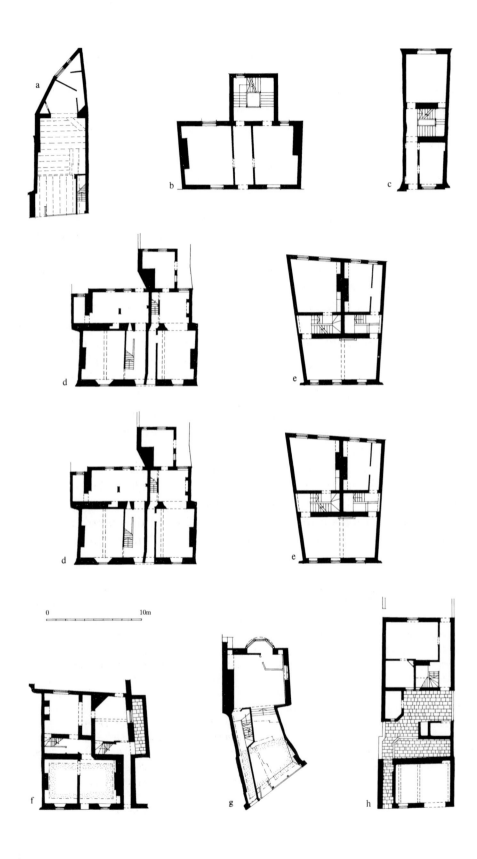

a

b

c

d

e

d

e

0   10m

f

g

h

framed tenements on the same plot. When enlargement was necessary, as at 22 Allergate, the additional rooms were incorporated into a rear wing or a full range running parallel with the street, so creating the double pile house plan, popular in new buildings from the seventeenth century onwards (**46**).

Where space within a burgage plot was limited, extension upwards was common. When the late medieval house at 3 Owengate, built hard against the castle wall, was remodelled around 1700, the builders thriftily reinstated the late medieval roof timbers above the new second floor. The process of extension and renewal often led to the rebuilding of the original medieval frontage building after a rear extension had been added. This creates a form of alternate development, in which the rear block predates the front range as at 8 Saddler Street.

The pressure for redevelopment at the outer edges of the medieval town led to the subdivisions of broad plot frontages. At 33/34 South Street, a simple two-roomed seventeenth-century cottage was subdivided around 1800 with pretty twin doorcases and each part given new rear extensions (**57**). In the centre of town where burgage plots were already narrow, the pressure to build was greatest and second houses were often built at the rear of the plot, separated by a courtyard and accessible from the front via the vennel, creating a back-plot development. In Saddler Street the courtyard between the houses at numbers 73-75 was infilled last century to extend the shop while, at 4 North Bailey, the rear house retains its separate identity and canopied front door.

Within the medieval burgage plots there was therefore great scope for extension and rebuilding. However, in the narrowest plots, the pressure to expand often led to the acquisition of neighbouring plots and the amalgamation of the buildings upon them. These are readily identifiable by their broad frontages in the densest urban areas of the Bishop's Borough, principally in

56 *House plans – all ground floor except (e). (a) 32 Silver Street: early seventeenth-century, timber-framed front block with shop entry and side entry to first floor. Longer range to rear, ground floor gutted by twentieth-century retail expansion. (b) 45/46 Saddler Street: broad plot development of late seventeenth-century new building with rear stair wing (entrance shown restored). (c) 40 Saddler Street: narrow plot development of late seventeenth century with mid-eighteenth-century central staircase and early nineteenth-century façade. (d) 33/34 South Street: plot division c.1800, of a broad frontage seventeenth-century cottage to create two houses, each with rear extensions. (e) 38/39 Saddler Street (first floor): amalgamation of two seventeenth-century house plots in the mid-eighteenth century, creating a fine front saloon. (f) Dun Cow Cottage: division and reunification – a complex plan originating as a single broad frontage property, with cellar (stippled), later divided in the eighteenth century and now one house again. (g) 8 Saddler Street: alternate development – medieval frontage building with rear extension c.1660-70. Frontage redeveloped c.1800 possibly a Paving Commissioner's realignment, preserving vestiges of the former house in the cellar. (h) 72 Hallgarth Street: tandem development – a rare example in one of the city's outer streets. Late medieval single storey cottage to front, later seventeenth- and eighteenth-century house rebuilt behind, with shared vennel entry*

57 *33/34 South Street is an example of a broad frontage house subdivided and extended, the adjoining front doors sharing a common elliptical-arched surround.* Graeme Stearman

Saddler Street. Numbers 38/39 (seventeenth- and eighteenth-century), 41/42 (early eighteenth-century) and 43/44 (mid-eighteenth century) all represent this process (**58**). Confusingly, numbers 45/46 and 47/48, though similar in appearance and size, in fact represent respectively a late seventeenth-century new building (across the castle moat?) and an early nineteenth-century assembly room on the site of the North Gate.

Such acquisition of adjoining plots did lead to the construction of houses designed to a uniform architectural character. Durham has a number of examples, most notably the impressive early eighteenth-century group of three houses at 46-49 Old Elvet. More frequently larger terraces were built on undeveloped land during the early to mid-nineteenth century: 21-32 Hallgarth Street (*c.*1843), Leazes Place (*c.*1840), 116-130 Gilesgate (early nineteenth-century), Crossgate, Neville Street and Castle Chare (mid-nineteenth-century) and Colpitts Terrace (1856).

58 *41/42 Saddler Street. The broad façade of this early eighteenth-century building, with its fine late Victorian shop front, disguises its origins as two separate houses, evident in its independent early cellars, two floors below street level.* Graeme Stearman

Materials

Timber-framed construction continued as a declining tradition in Durham well into the seventeenth century, by which time brick had begun to be identified as the basic material for post-Restoration rebuilding. Certainly the carpentry of early seventeenth-century houses such as 32 Silver Street is less impressive than earlier examples. Brick had been used here to infill the timber-framed panels, although it had appeared earlier in the castle kitchens (1499) and at Kepier Hospital (after 1588) where it is constructed in the locally rare English bond.

The earlier 50mm bricks (2in) thicken slightly in the later eighteenth century, before standardising at around 70 mm (2¾in), probably after the brick tax in 1784. The most common bond in the city is English garden wall bond, with Flemish bond introduced later, for example at St Godric's Court (the former Castle Chare Arts Centre) rear wing (*c.*1750-60). Sandstone was always

135

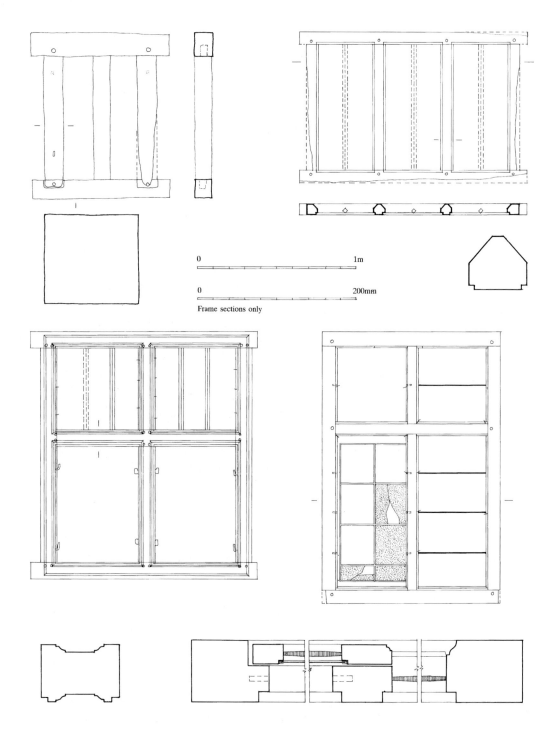

59 *Early windows (external view). 11 Silver Street – unglazed, but shuttered; fifteenth century (above left). 80 Saddler Street – glazed; sixteenth or early seventeenth century (above right). 8 Saddler Street – top lights glazed, bottom lights shuttered; c.1660-70 (below left). 20 South Bailey – fully glazed casement, later modified for horizontal sash; c.1700 (below right)*

0   1m

0   200mm

Frame sections only

the material for the highest quality buildings in the city. It was used in domestic buildings alongside brick in the seventeenth and eighteenth centuries and enjoyed a modest revival in the early to mid-nineteenth century in such humble terraces as Crossgate, Neville Street, Castle Chare and Gilesgate where, at number 128, magnesian limestone – the stone of the eastern half of the county – is seen in pleasing juxtaposition with traditional brick and sandstone façades.

It was also traditional to cover the wall construction in a lime render. Early coverings have been found trapped behind late construction at 70 Saddler Street where seventeenth-century pebble-dashing was revealed. Eighteenth- and early nineteenth-century renders are more often smooth-finished, latterly with ashlar scoring used in imitation of stonework. Render usually protects poor materials or disguises unsightly alterations but in the early nineteenth century it was fashionable in its own right, as seen at 53-55 Old Elvet. Walls were generally bonded with lime mortar in this period, replacing the clay binders used in simpler dwellings in the medieval period.

Early domestic roof coverings in Durham would have been straw, reed and black (heather) thatch with stone slates for the better houses. Clay pantiles came first from the Low Countries and have no certain date of intro- duction in Durham, though late seventeenth century is likely. They gradually replaced thatch and are often found with a stone slate verge, a local variant of debatable origins, as at 54-56 Hallgarth Street. Westmorland slates, laid like stone slates in diminishing courses, appear occasionally at the vernacular level of the modest townhouse from the late eighteenth century onwards. With the coming of the railways, Welsh slate assumed its gradual dominance in the city.

External features

Architectural variety was not monopolised by the great men in Durham's history. Even the most humble citizens wanted their houses to be as comfort- able and as fashionable as their means would allow. If rebuilding and extensions were too costly, refacading was often undertaken. More modestly, older windows were replaced with new sashes and, if nothing else, the front doorway, still a most potent symbol of fashion, was improved. Consequently, early windows are rare in Durham and usually survive beneath rendering, probably blocked in response to the window tax introduced in 1696 and raised throughout the eighteenth century until its repeal in 1851 (**59**).

Casements of late sixteenth- or early seventeenth-century date survive in the rear house at 75 Saddler Street, with richly moulded mullions and transoms. Much simpler chamfered designs were used in 80 Saddler Street and added to the medieval sidewall of 11 Silver Street. In the late seventeenth century, the cross-window was introduced and appears in stone on the ground floor and in timber above at 8 Saddler Street. A better proportioned and refined design at 20 South Bailey marks the transition between fixed leaded light and the introduction of horizontal sliding sashes (*c.*1700–1720).

The first vertical sash window appeared in the early to mid-eighteenth century in Durham, multi-paned with thick glazing bars at first, many replaced with much thinner bars in the early nineteenth century. They were proposed at Croxdale in 1704, regionally a very early date, and installed with some difficulty at Newton Hall in 1723, replacing the cross window originally planned in the 1717 design for the house. The house at 3 South Bailey (*c.*1720) displays both early and later glazing bars types in its façade, with little loss of balance (**50**). By the mid-nineteenth century, despite the availability of larger glass panes for more prestigious houses, at the vernacular level the traditional 12- and 16-paned sash window was still used in Durham, as at Colpitts Terrace in 1856.

Doorways on domestic buildings in the late seventeenth century usually echoed the traditional four-centred head design in either stone or wood. The difficulties of stylistic dating are best exemplified on Palace Green, admittedly non-domestic, where Cosin placed a traditional Tudor doorway in his almshouses (1666) and the following year constructed an entire baroque

60 *2 South Bailey. A reconstruction as built c.1670 (left) and as heightened and remodelled in the late eighteenth century (right)*

doorcase in his library. Much simpler entrances of the period placed the fashionable bulls-eye over an arched surround as a proto-fanlight, as at Crook Hall (1671) and 2 South Bailey (**60**). By the eighteenth century, arched surrounds had largely disappeared, displaced by square architraves usually with a bulbous bolection moulding. A more impressive effect was achieved with the addition of ornate brackets and a straight cornice or pediment, as at Abbey House, Palace Green. By the later eighteenth century, fanlights were common, rectangular or semi-circular, the latter often breaking into the pediment above (**colour plate 18**). This is the design of the doorcases at 199/200 Gilesgate, where the Gothic influence is evident in their slender shafted pilasters. Perhaps the finest early nineteenth-century surround is 25 North Bailey where the fanlight dictates the form of the deep arched reveal with fluted doorcase of around 1820.

Doors generally survive from the late seventeenth century. Early internal examples with two raised and fielded panels and bolection moulds are common. The Georgian six panel door is standard throughout the town with the bottom two panels usually solid except when used internally. With the arrival of Adam's classical influences in the late eighteenth century, reed panels with paterae in the angles appear.

Internal features

Surviving internal features in domestic buildings rarely pre-date the late seventeenth century. There are roof spaces and basements with a few late sixteenth/seventeenth-century fragments of wainscot panelling and doors, complete with contemporary ironmongery. Some are *in situ* (e.g. 73 Saddler Street), some have been exiled from the principal living accommodation when fashion made them embarrassingly outmoded as at 22 Allergate. So attics are always worth exploring.

Staircases were utilitarian and cramped in medieval houses. Between 1560 and 1660, none has survived in Durham, all replaced from the late seventeenth century onwards when the staircase was given a new prominence in Durham houses, a fashion stimulated by Cosin's Black Stairs in the castle. This staircase must have been very influential in its day and spawned a number of vernacular examples such as that in Dun Cow Cottage, now in 6a The College of around 1670. These late seventeenth-century staircases occupied a central position in the house-plan, where they were meant to impress. They succeeded most spectacularly when they were designed around an open well, rising from basement to attic, as seen at 45/46 Saddler Street, around 1680 (**61**). They were usually made of painted pine, though one of the most powerful stairs at 12 South Bailey is in oak. Balustrades were characteristically strong and robust, with closed strings, close set balusters often of bine twist design with a high and heavy handrail. At the corners of each flight, newel posts were usually panelled with ball finials above and pendant drops below. Into the eighteenth century, designs were lightened, balusters were tapered and slender, handrails were smaller and dogleg stairs became the most popular plan.

The position of the staircase was given even greater prominence in two eighteenth-century examples in the Bailey. The Eden house, 3 South Bailey (*c*.1720) introduced a much lighter stair, rising though only one floor but set as a show piece in the main entrance hall. The balusters were thin and delicately carved – a rarity in Durham. The string was open to display the tread ends with carved spandrel pieces below them. Along the street at 24 North Bailey, (*c*.1760) the entire well stair with a continuous moulded handrail was made the focus of the classical entrance hall, the whole lit by a large Venetian window above the front door.

Next door, number 25, exemplifies the best qualities of the early nineteenth-century Durham staircases, graceful and light with a slender mahogany rail set on plain balusters. The continuity of the rail between floors, without

61 *The staircase of 45/46 Saddler Street displays typical details of late seventeenth-century staircases in Durham – a broad handrail, bine twist or 'barley sugar' balusters and a closed string.* City of Durham Council

62 *The fine early seventeenth-century ceiling at 80 Saddler Street.* City of Durham Council

newels, created a most beautiful sense of space. The typical late seventeenth-century fireplace was stone-arched and set in a moulded square surround, for instance 8 Saddler Street (*c.*1670). Gradually the arch disappeared in favour of the bolection mould. Both are present in a fireplace at 19 North Bailey (*c.*1700), the arch being minimal in the extreme.

The most ambitious mid-eighteenth-century designs supported a carved overmantel, which formed part of the architectural composition of a panelled or plasterwork interior, as at 36/37 Saddler Street. A large number of panelled rooms survives mainly from the late seventeenth to mid-eighteenth centuries. Their designs again echo the developing trend from heavier joinery sections to thinner mouldings and a general lightness of touch. The first floor drawing room in the Georgian wing at Crook Hall (*c.*1736) is one of the most elegant examples.

Plasterwork in room interiors is usually eighteenth-century and is limited to cornice decoration, central roses and panelwork above a timber dado. Three exceptional examples, however, deserve special mention. In 80 Saddler Street is a very rare, richly decorated ceiling, dating from the early years of the seventeenth century. Between a pattern of moulded ribs the panels contain a variety of individual flower motifs. It has been suggested that this may be the work of John Johnstoun, a Yorkshire plasterer who was travelling north to Scotland undertaking commissions as he went (**62**).

In the mid-eighteenth century, the fashion for sumptuous Rococo plasterwork in room interiors was adopted in two city houses that form part of a wider regional group. In St Godric's Court (the former Castle Chare Arts

141

Centre), the 'Green Room' contains exceptional plasterwork over all surfaces. At Aykley Heads House, just north of the city, a smaller room is no less intensively decorated. Both have fine chimney pieces with carved overmantles. They belong to a group of such interiors near the city: Coxhoe Hall (after 1749, now destroyed), Elemore Hall (1752 and 1757) and Croxdale Hall (1766). All this local Rococo plasterwork may well be the work of the Italian stuccoist Giuseppe Cortese, who is known from documents to have executed the work at Elemore and Croxdale (**colour plate 17**).

6
PARKS AND GARDENS

Landscape and architecture are inseparable in Durham. Just as the buildings of the city have endured countless repairs and modifications to their fabric, so too the open spaces between them – the gardens, parks and riverbanks – have been adapted to reflect changes in function and fashion.

Medieval gardens

The evidence for medieval gardens in Durham lies predominantly in documents. On the ground, little survives beyond much repaired boundary walls. Those of the town can be quickly considered. Tenement gardens in the Bishop's Borough are noted in 1388, many cited as 'under the moat', presumably in Silver Street and Saddler Street. Two outside Kingsgate were 'on the Waste', the flat land below the present St Chad's College. Their primary purpose would be for food production – vegetables, herbs and possibly fruit – as well as for medicinal and decorative reasons. Beyond the town more space was available, and the ancient walls surrounding Crook Hall may well enclose parts of its medieval gardens.

Within the bishop's castle, space for gardens would, at first, have been limited. The motte and the apron below the walls were cleared of vegetation for defensive reasons. The courtyard would be even more cluttered with buildings than at present, and formal gardens may have been little more than pocket handkerchief private lawns, such as those laid out for royalty in the Edwardian castles of North Wales. The decline in the castle's military role in the late medieval period may well have been reflected in greater space being found for gardens in the redundant earthworks, but the documentary or archaeological evidence for this is still lacking.

Fortunately there is a much greater survival of documentary evidence for the priory gardens. The monastic buildings occupied a very restricted site at the end of the peninsula, and to provide the necessary gardens and orchards to support the monastery required large cultivated areas on the neighbouring banks.

Like all the great monastic houses, Durham had several gardens and these were in the control of individual priory officers or obedientiaries. The cellarer had a large walled garden across the Wear in the Old Borough between

63 *The priory's west orchard was annexed to St Margaret's churchyard in the nineteenth century and now serves as an invaluable open space for the surrounding community.* Graeme Stearman

Crossgate and South Street, now St Margaret's churchyard extension and allotments (**63**). There were various enclosures known as the West Garden, West Orchard, Ympgarth and Hoglyn. Beside the production of vegetables and fruit, there were also fishponds, stocked with pike in 1469-70, and a dovecot.

The hostillar's walled garden is recorded in the fifteenth century within his manor farm at Elvethall in Hallgarth Street, while the almoner kept an orchard to the south-west of the peninsula and gardens attached to his hospital of St Mary Magdalene in Gilesgate. By comparison with other monastic sites, the walled garden of the infirmary master would have been particularly important, providing him with many of the medicinal herbs needed to aid the treatment of convalescent brethren. Its location is unknown, it could have been south of the College, the monastery's outer court, enclosed within the precinct wall. It may have had a formally planned central lawn with grass walks, as turf was required for gardening work there in the early fifteenth century. The herb beds may have surrounded the lawn, perhaps with a central pond fed by the piped water supply referred to in accounts in 1422-3.

This fragrant garden was, no doubt, popular with the monks as was the small terraced enclosure beside the dormitory known as the Monks Bowling Green. Such were their attractions that complaints were made to the bishop in 1442 that, after evening prayers, the monks were enjoying the long summer evenings laughing and talking in the gardens, instead of retiring to bed.

Post-medieval gardens

At the Reformation, the three great religious estates in the city suffered varying fates. The bishopric was maintained and the priory dissolved and its property re-endowed to the new Dean and Chapter. Only Kepier Hospital underwent complete suppression in 1545 with the dispersal of its personnel and the sale of its land. The early owners did little with the estate until John Heath, a successful London merchant, acquired Kepier in 1555, but a sitting tenant prevented his moving to the property until 1568. His home at Kepier would most probably have been an adaptation of the old medieval infirmary hall with its adjacent chapel which, added to the other redundant hospital buildings, provided an ample suite of rooms for John Heath and his son and grandson, both John, who succeeded to the estate. The physical evidence of the surviving buildings suggests the Heaths at least re-roofed the gatehouse and provided it with new external stairs to the first floor.

Towards the end of the sixteenth century, probably after 1590, the grandson of John Heath of London, known for matters of clarity as John Heath II of Kepier, laid out the great walled garden south of the medieval hospital precinct. The garden was a broadly rectangular enclosure bordering the riverside approach to the gatehouse. Along its northern boundary, centrally aligned on the flatter western part of the garden, was a brick banqueting house set above a fashionable Italian loggia. This building has long been identified as the Heath's new house but the documentary evidence of its four elevations shows that, when first built, it stood alone, its accommodation only a single room on each floor over a garden loggia, accessible by a fine oak staircase. One can imagine that John Heath found it frustrating to lay out his new garden, quite one of the best in the city at the time, yet neither he nor his guests could enjoy it from the cluttered confinement of his medieval hospital buildings. How much more impressive to take his dinner guests out to the nearby banqueting house, set out perhaps for pre-prandial drinks or post-prandial desserts, to admire from the first floor room the expansive proportions of his walled garden and the pleasing symmetry of his planting. The subsequent owners of the Kepier estate, the Cole family, appreciated this building and after the Restoration, probably before 1669, added fine 'Cosin' panelling to the main room.

Celia Fiennes visited Durham in the summer of 1698, when the Musgrave family owned Kepier but never lived there. The gardens were given over to public amenity by then and she noted that although the house (probably the medieval hospital buildings) was in ruins, 'the gardens are flourishing still with good walks and much fruite of which I tasted. It is a place that is used like our Spring Gardens for the company of the town to walk in the evenings and its most pleasant by the river'.

By the date of her visit, the walled garden at Kepier would have been supplemented by a narrow riverside terrace, set against the high wall of the Heath garden, adorned with espaliered fruit. Her description strongly implied that she walked along it, looking over a low wall to the view of the flowing river close by. The earlier Heath garden, though large, was enclosed by high walls; the garden experience was within the walls, the river was largely ignored. The new riverside terrace added an external view that was closely reflected in other city gardens of the seventeenth century. One such, at Old Durham, was the product of yet another member of the 'green fingered' Heath family.

Old Durham lies 1.5km (1 mile) to the east of the city centre and in the late medieval period became a part of the Kepier Hospital estate, subsequently sold to John Heath of London. His descendant John Heath IV of Kepier, inherited it in 1630 and from that date he most probably began the construction of the locally renowned 'hanging gardens' to the east of his old manor house (64). Work may have continued after the Civil War and certainly the central gazebo bore the initials of John Heath IV, who died in 1665. The gazebo was subsequently modified from rectangular form to a square, with raised walls and a pyramidal roof. The fine corner alcove closely resembles the Crook Hall examples, so dating the remodelling to around 1730-40. Not long after, the manor house was demolished, but the gardens seem to have been maintained, for part of the time at least, during the middle years of the eighteenth century. In 1748, Mrs Jane Thackray announced the continuance of the nursery gardens at Old Durham, following the recent death of her husband John Forest and fruit trees, shrubs, flowering plants and bulbs were all for sale. In 1753, the gardens were being used for a choir concert, a public amenity praised later in the century (1787) by William Hutchinson:

> This sweet retirement has become a place of public resort, where concerts of music have frequently been performed in the summer evenings, and the company regaled with fruit, tea, etc.

By the mid-nineteenth century, the garden house was converted into a public house called 'The Pine Apple' that retained its licence until earlier last century when once again the gardens were abandoned. Their remains, and those of its ruined gazebo, were bought by the City Council in 1985. Old Durham has now undergone archaeological excavation, restoration and replanting to seventeenth- and eighteenth-century designs.

The site lies on the west-facing slope of the river valley with two upper walled gardens united by the gazebo, that in turn presides centrally over the

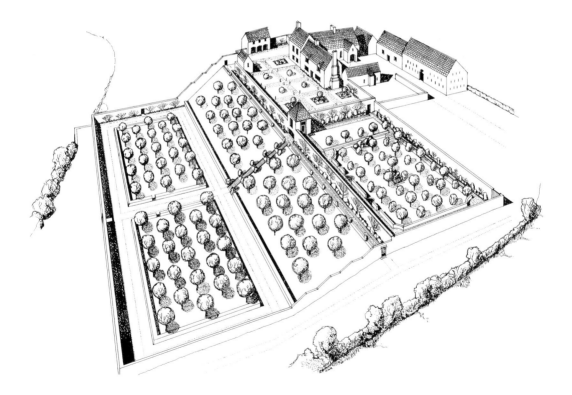

64 *Old Durham Gardens as they may have appeared in the early years of the eighteenth century, at the height of their development and before their temporary abandonment. This drawing is based upon the writings of John Parkinson, whereas the executed planting in the lower garden is based upon the writings of William Lawson*

long terrace with its flight of stone steps leading down into the lower walled garden. In the north–east corner was the manor house, now almost completely vanished. It is surely no coincidence that this was aligned precisely on the axial eastern view of the cathedral, a view so enjoyable from the long terrace walk.

The three enclosures may originally have been conceived as the flower and kitchen gardens on the upper level and the orchard below, in the manner advocated at the time by John Parkinson in *Paradisi in Sole, Paradisus Terrestris* (1629). Subsequent research by Fiona Green considered the more local author, William Lawson, likely to be a stronger influence through his books, *The Country House-Wife's Garden* (1617) and *A New Orchard and Garden* (1618). The orchard garden has been reconstructed by Fiona Green in accordance with his recommendations. Excavations in the southern upper garden, however, revealed a formal layout of tree pits enclosed within hedge trenches and wall borders. There were central and axial flowerbeds and small ponds too. The whole garden was destroyed for a new bowling green, probably laid out in the early nineteenth century. Reconstruction of the original seventeenth-century formal layout here was not possible due to later walling realignments and so the upper garden planting evokes the form of the garden as it may have appeared after the remodelling of the gazebo in the early eighteenth century.

There is a hint, no more, in the gardens of Old Durham that their construction may have been interrupted by the events of the Civil War and the Interregnum. This is hardly surprising and the disruption was nowhere more keenly felt than on the peninsula. The works of reconstruction on the castle and cathedral, undertaken by John Cosin after the Restoration of Charles II and his own elevation to the bishopric in 1660, have been referred to in previous chapters. His garden works, though less well known, were executed with the same single-mindedness of purpose.

In the Castle it is clear that, on the completion of major building works and the erection of a fine lead-lined fountain in the courtyard in 1664, Cosin turned his attention to the creation of new gardens (**65**). His improvements recognise the final abandonment of the castle's military role and nothing symbolised this change of attitude better than the demolition of the cramped medieval barbican in 1665. It was rebuilt as a generous forecourt and the adjacent moat levelled to form new gardens. Towards the end of the same year the castle motte beneath Bishop Hatfield's abandoned keep was terraced in three levels and in February 1666, Thomas Miller was paid 'for turfing the walkes under the great tower' (**15**). A little later 56 rose trees and 24 gooseberry trees were planted respectively on the banks and in the 'new walks'. This garden work may have extended to the bastion tower between the castle and the North Gate, which led onto the new North Terrace (**12**). The newly-created moat gardens, the present Fellows' and Master's gardens either side of the barbican, most probably served as an orchard and kitchen garden as John Usher was 'setting pease' there in May 1667 (**8**).

65 *The late seventeenth-century gardens of Bishop Cosin were formed out of the obsolete castle earthworks. The old Norman motte was terraced with three walks, work starting probably in the autumn of 1665 and completed ready for spring planting early the following year.* Graeme Stearman

One final garden, called the Bishop's Walk, is delightfully recorded in early eighteenth-century paintings, complete it would seem with walking bishops. Sadly it is poorly represented in the documents. It lay south-west of the castle below the castle wall. A long terrace walk with formal planting was set out here, bounded by crenellated brick walls with stone dressings. Rising above it was a tall octagonal tower with a well-lit upper chamber, an early belvedere, aligned on Cosin's new library and looking out over the river below. Were these the 'battlement' and 'mount' referred to in the bishop's accounts in 1667? The vestiges remain of the enclosing walls, the site of the tower acknowledged by the angled projection of the castle wall (**15**). The garden itself remains an overgrown and neglected wasteland awaiting restoration.

Cosin's work in the castle was no doubt an exemplar and a catalyst for the improvement of much of the city. The condition of the prebendal houses in the College were, after the Interregnum, no better than the castle to judge by the renovation and rebuilding undertaken during the late seventeenth and early eighteenth centuries. Formal gardens would be laid out in imitations of the bishop's work and around 1680, Prebends Walk was constructed along a length of the medieval castle walls that had collapsed.

The essential ingredients of a large terraced walk, a sloping site beneath and an outward prospect over flowing water, link Bishop's and Prebends Walks back to John Heath IV's new garden at Old Durham. Before he departed from

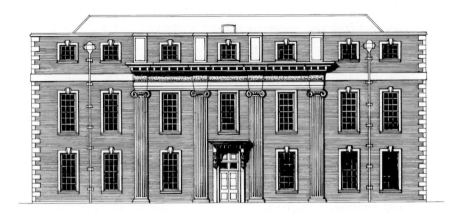

66 *Newton Hall: the west façade of the remodelled house of 1717-23*

the city to Old Durham, John lived in the buildings now occupied by Hatfield College in North Bailey. The unusual position of these buildings against the castle wall, not along the Bailey, demand far more research than they have received to date. From Bok's illustration (**6**) there was a substantial tower house here by the late seventeenth century. The ability to view the riverbanks directly from the house was a unique situation for Bailey houses and might suggest that, once the riverbanks began to be tamed by terraces and gardens, this may have been an early example. The flat terrace below the wall was present in the 1850s – might it have been a much earlier creation?

The seventeenth-century gardens of Durham deserve deeper study. Seen in a national context they reflect the prevailing fashion for formality in design, long terraces with planned panoramas from gazebo or tower. These were city gardens looking out to the natural landscape of the riverbanks. As we have seen at Old Durham, there were gardens outside the city that looked in to the cathedral, using it as a focal point, an eye-catcher, in their designs. Newton Hall was such a garden landscape.

Newton Hall stood on high ground about a mile north of the city, thereby ensuring it crept into most eighteenth century panoramas of the peninsula, albeit in minuscule form. Newton was an ancient settlement, mentioned in the Boldon Book of 1183. The estate was owned by many of the great Durham families – Bowes, Middleton and Blakiston. Shortly after the Restoration it was sold to another important family – the Liddells. They acquired a medieval manor house and perhaps the vestiges of an old village, but of its early gardens we know nothing.

Sir Henry Liddell (*c.*1644-1723) was one of the prime movers in attempts to regulate the north-east coal trade in the early eighteenth century and alongside his business interests he planned the reconstruction of his two

County Durham estates at Newton Hall and Ravensworth Castle, near Gateshead. He set down his thoughts in letters to his son John, debating the subtleties of sash windows or garden parterres, or railing against the builders' delays. Newton Hall was restored around 1717-23. The main rebuilding was completed by 1717 but the installation of new sash windows was still taking place in 1723 (**66**). His gardens extended west and south of the Hall, the main western aspect being along the great avenue. Bounded by woodland north and south, this avenue was constructed by cutting a deep wide trough through rising ground to frame the prospects out from and into the Hall. Sir Henry proposed to construct a rondpoint at the end of this avenue, a viewpoint from which further radiating avenues were cut through the woodland along the eight points of the compass to landmarks such as Kepier Hospital, Gateshead windmills and, of course, Durham Cathedral. It is not known if this ambitious scheme was ever executed (**67**).

The formality of the great avenue was reflected in the large and ornate parterre that was laid out in front of the south façade. Sir Henry commissioned a design for this walled garden in 1718 and discussed with his son the need for raised walks around the formal beds. This very formal design, with its clipped

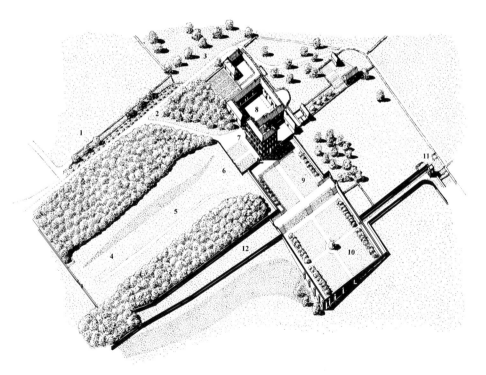

67 *A bird's eye view of Newton Hall and its grounds as it may have looked in the middle of the nineteenth century. Key: (1) Fishponds (2) Carriage drive (3) Copse (4) Rondpoint (site of) (5) Avenue (6) West front of Hall (7) Hall (8) Service yard (9) Parterre (10) Lower garden (11) Gazebo (12) Terrace*

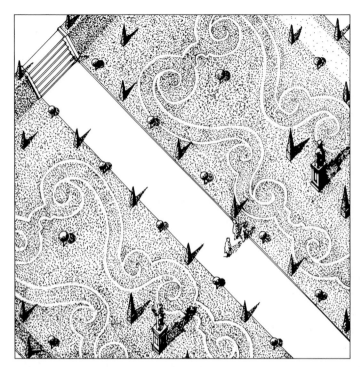

68 *The parterre at Newton Hall as it would have appeared c.1723*

pyramidal yew and ornately patterned beds, drew its inspiration from the influential King's Privy Garden executed at Hampton Court Palace some sixteen years earlier (**68**). The Newton Hall parterre was not therefore an innovative design and closely resembled another formal garden drawn at Brancepeth Castle in 1728. The revolution in English landscape design, that swept away formal parterres in favour of the informality of the natural landscape, was still some years away.

Sir Henry's parterre looked south but the view from the Hall was enclosed, blinkered by high walls east and west. The finest panorama was of course to the south too, towards the cathedral, and to view this, the eighteenth-century visitor would have passed through the parterre to take the west end gate through the high wall, out onto a long terrace set high above the sloping fields below. This was a landscape feature that Sir Henry may have inherited from others. After the relative confinement of the walled gardens, the view from this vantage point must have been breathtaking. Here was the culmination of a promenade around the gardens with its climax in the distant eye-catcher of Durham Cathedral.

Sir Henry Liddell's Newton Hall and gardens were removed in the major house building of the 1960s. But, like dandelions through tarmac, history has a way of poking through the most destructive efforts of modern developers. Despite the carpet of residential development across the Newton Hall estate, traces of the eighteenth-century estate remain in the carriage drive, the vestiges of service buildings, old brick walls and the gentle dip of the great avenue. The evidence is nowhere stronger than at the narrow shelf of land on which the long terrace was laid out, still the best vantage point in the area. Where the visitor today looks down on the cathedral in its woodland setting, Sir Henry would have gazed at this eye-catcher set upon the treeless riverbanks that were to undergo great transformations during the next century.

The riverbanks

The wooded gorge of the River Wear, making its long meander around the peninsula at Durham, is a great deception. This is not the relict landscape of some primeval forest, but a complex pattern of natural recolonisation and planned planting upon the modified topography of the riverbanks. Durham was chosen as the final resting-place of St Cuthbert because of its naturally fortified position, the river acting as a moat to the peninsula fortress. From the earliest occupation, it was essential to keep the banks below the castle walls free from all vegetation to ensure an open view for the garrison.

The construction of the Anglo-Saxon cathedral, and the later and more extensive Norman building campaigns, required vast quantities of local stone, and the exposed sandstone on the cliff sides of the river gorge enabled easy and accessible quarrying. This would have occurred first on the peninsula itself; later, particularly after the construction of Framwellgate Bridge, the left bank opposite the peninsula would be quarried, where operations were not constrained by the buildings above. Only at St Oswald's did the early church and churchyard prevent quarrying and so preserve the original gorge cliffs (**1**).

Quarries were owned by all the overlords and by private citizens as well. The priory had most, mainly on the south and west sides below South Street, where the Sacrist's Quarry survives as the Dell near Prebends Bridge. Throughout the medieval period, the castle and priory had garderobes and reredorters discharging their human effluent onto the banks and so into the river. Most of the townspeople with ready access to the banks or bridges would have done likewise, regarding the river as an open sewer.

During the sixteenth and seventeenth centuries, quarrying on the river-banks began to decline with improved transportation from better quarries further afield and, as they were abandoned, trees and shrubs recolonised the left bank of the river. Despite the final expiration of the castle's defensive role, the banks below the castle appear to have stayed free of significant vegetation. In 1696, St Cuthbert's Well was constructed and marks an early improvement on the riverbanks. Celia Fiennes, visiting Durham two years later, also noted that 'the walks are very pleasant by the riverside'.

The turn of the eighteenth century is a convenient place to discuss the development of private Bailey gardens on the peninsula banks. The limited incursion of Bishop's and Prebends' Walks outside the castle walls and onto the riverbanks have been described and the possibility of an early garden at Hatfield College has been considered. How did the gardens of North and South Baileys develop beyond their castle wall boundaries? There were always 'closes' below the castle wall even in medieval times. These were probably walled or fenced areas of flatter ground on the east and south side of the peninsula, where some cultivation could be carried out, accessible through the Kingsgate or Watergate postern. The formation of direct links between upper rear Bailey gardens and the correspondingly narrow plots below the castle wall, which were extensions of the burgage plots, might broadly be said to have taken place in the period 1660-1750.

By the mid-eighteenth century a number of southern panoramas of the city display the sweeping apron of narrow terraced riverbank gardens, admired by their owners from gazebos and belvederes atop the castle wall. This process of extension probably took place along the whole length of the Bailey, but this can only be an assumption given the scarcity of contemporary illustrations of the peninsula from the east. Over the following century, from 1750-1850, the Bailey riverbank gardens remain in cultivation but undergo further transformations that result in the wonderfully detailed first edition Ordnance Survey maps of 1857 that provide such rich material for analysis. Much of that research is still to be done. For example how were the gardens south of Bow Lane (modern St Chad's College) actually used? The layout of paths indicates part-private and part-communal areas within the narrow but interlinked gardens.

The maps provide considerable detail. They reveal the formality of many of the gardens focussed on ponds, fountains or statuary, with paths leading through the castle wall to bankside icehouses set in more wooded areas. Informal flower beds are also shown, and it is sobering to think that the gardener's modest labours in setting out a small bed of roses on the Monday might be recorded for posterity by the team of Royal Engineers surveyors who arrived on the Tuesday.

The most notable feature of the Bailey gardens in 1857 was the great garden of the Bowes family house (4 South Bailey), the result of extensive amalgamation of lower garden plots to create a space worthy of landscape gardening on a grand scale. The broad and long terraced walk (now the Principal's Walk of St John's College) overlooks narrow paths cutting down diagonally across the slope towards the river's edge. The effect of this expansion was to deny many Bailey householders the chance to enjoy the lower slopes, their predecessors having presumably sold, leased or sub-let their land to the acquisitive Bowes family. This was a problem faced by the Shipperdsons who, probably in the early nineteenth century (c.1820–30) found their lower garden formed the southern end of the great Bowes terrace. They appear to have created a path across the end of their neighbour's upper garden along the top of the castle wall, which then descends into their own generous grounds, a dislocated plot some distance from their house. These grounds they beautified with informal planting, an icehouse with an Egyptian or Mycenean tomb-portal and a gardener's cottage designed as a classical Greek temple (The Count's House), possibly a design by Ignatius Bonomi (**71**). The informality of their planting was by this time reflecting the broader informality of the woodland planting of the riverbanks, and the story of that wider landscape should now resume.

Analysis of those eighteenth-century engravings that so splendidly illustrate the Bailey gardens also highlight the gradual afforestation of the banks, particularly on the western side below the castle and cathedral (**69**). The cathedral prebend, Dr Joseph Spence, an accomplished garden designer and friend of Alexander Pope, was one of the first to introduce new paths and tree planting

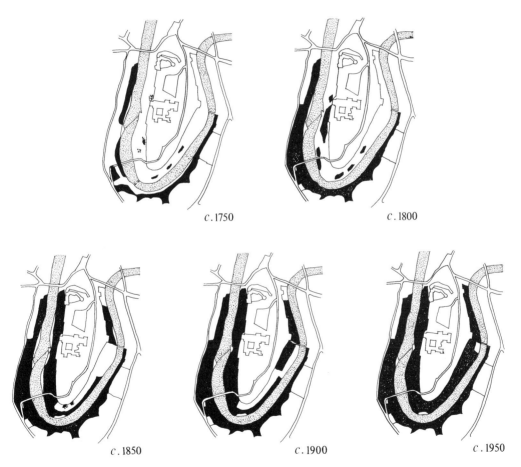

c.1750   *c*.1800

c.1850   *c*.1900   *c*.1950

69 *Tree cover on the riverbanks from 1750 to 1950. The recolonisation of abandoned quarries on the left bank of the river was evident from an early date, with only sporadic planting on the peninsula itself, where planned planting from the mid-eighteenth century onwards gradually developed the mature tree canopy. From the end of the last century the cover has been supplemented more from the recolonisation of abandoned gardens than from any deliberate strategy*

70 *The classic view of the cathedral, above the River Wear: a planned landscape setting of comparatively recent date.* City of Durham Council

during his residency, 1754-68. The eighteenth-century 'improvers' in Durham saw in the riverbanks all the components that create the classic Romantic landscape – dramatic site, ancient buildings and water – and only found it lacking in trees. Undertaking tree planting was therefore a far easier task than that of other contemporary landscape designers, who had to import water, create the topography and usually build the ruins or temple too. Whatever practical considerations led to the siting of the new Prebends Bridge after the flood of 1771 had swept away the old bridge, its new position in the landscape garden of the riverbanks was perfect (**colour plate 21**). It offered the eighteenth-century visitor an unrivalled, and quite deliberate, panorama. Above the Arcadian Fulling Mill shrouded in woodland and washed by the River Wear, the ancient cathedral rose – the whole composition closed with a distant view of Framwellgate Bridge (**70**).

Into the emerging wooded landscape of the riverbanks, appropriate features were introduced during the eighteenth and early nineteenth centuries. The Count's House has been mentioned above, and this was supplemented by a number of well heads and springs that were all identified as points of interest on the perambulation. The whole scene was contemplated from the gardens and gazebos of the Bailey houses, set above the castle walls and towers. These ancient

156

walls were yet another feature in the landscape and, if they lacked a suitably medieval appearance, were embellished by new battlements (**71**). The peninsula tree planting included both native and non-native species – beech, oak, horse chestnut, sycamore, birch and willow were dominant, with lime, cherry, sweet chestnut, yew and some conifers being introduced (**colour plate 21**).

On the left bank, the recolonisation of abandoned quarries created a dramatic wooded landscape and led to some of William Hutchinson's most cloying prose (1787):

> Here the opening valley pours forth a rivulet, and there a solemn dell, with Nature's wildest beauties, yawns with rocks, which yield the living fountain from their lips, whilst each brow is crowded with bending oaks, whose naked talons and twisted arms rival each other in grotesque figure.

By the mid-nineteenth century, with the growing maturity of the tree canopy, the essential transformation of the riverbanks from defensive moat to one of the most treasured Romantic landscapes was complete.

The eighteenth and nineteenth centuries

There was little major landscaping work in Durham in the eighteenth century to equal the transformation of the riverbanks. In the College, Spence proposed an informal tree-planting scheme of Portuguese laurels, hollies, Virginia cedar and Virginia cypress. It is not known whether this was ever executed. The present planting appears more recent and reinforces the informality and serenity of the college. Palace Green seems always to have been largely treeless. Cosin saw fit to dig up its 'pible sand' and fill the holes with rubble. In the eighteenth century, if not before, an elongated octagonal area was grassed in the centre of it. This was only enlarged to its present size earlier last century.

Around the city, small country estates grew up, either developing from the older manor houses or new mansions and villas in their own parks and gardens. To the north-west of the centre was the Dryburn estate, home of W.L. Wharton in the mid-nineteenth century, the house now engulfed by the new University Hospital. Nearer to the city he established a summer garden on an exposed knoll overlooking the peninsula. He created a mock gun battery there to highlight the panorama (1858), and this has remained the focal point of Wharton Park since its bequest to the City Council.

A little further out lay the older estates of Aykley Heads and Newton Hall, already described, while along South Road new estates at Mount Oswald, Oswald House, Hollinside and Elvet Hill sprang up.

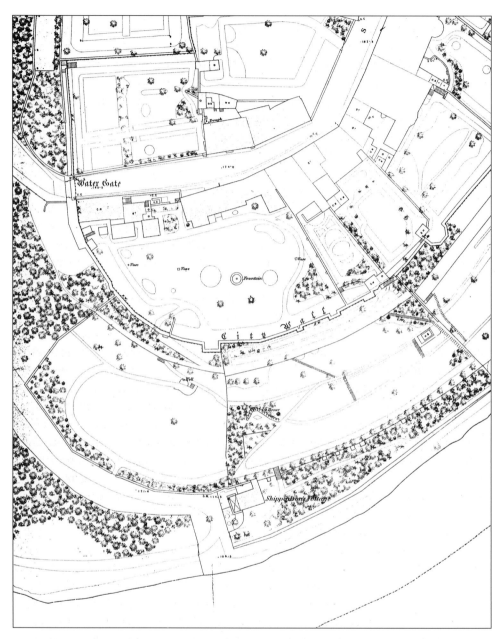

71 *The first edition of the Ordnance Survey map, showing the southern end of the peninsula (1857). The old medieval castle wall has terraces and summer houses laid out along its length. The steeply sloping banks below the walls are cultivated for gardens and their visitors' enjoyment of them was punctuated by such features as wells and springs, icehouses and, close to the water's edge, Shipperdson's Cottage, now known as The Count's House*

The twentieth century

In the last century it is the university, one of the city's new 'overlords', that has done most to create new parks and gardens in the city. The South Road colleges of Van Mildert and St Aidan's are particularly noteworthy, as is the focus of the university's horticultural work, the Botanic Gardens, established in 1970. These gardens, along with many of the South Road colleges, are all set within the mature landscape framework of the older nineteenth-century estates.

The Dean and Chapter's management of most of the riverbanks has in recent years extended to the siting of a number of sculptures by their artists-in-residence. In 1986-7, Colin Wilbourn sited two such works. These works are a logical development of the riverbanks' landscape history, and 'The Upper Room' was a brilliantly imaginative composition of thirteen elm trunks carved with a representation of the Last Supper (**colour plate 22**). This sculpture was always intended to be temporary, and so it proved to be. Despite generating considerable public affection, it suffered from the natural processes of timber decay, which led to its recent removal.

On the outer banks near Prebends Bridge, Richard Cole (cathedral artist-in-residence 1992-3) reassembled and pierced the old stonework of the north-east pinnacle of the Nine Altars to frame a view of the cathedral. The care and conservation of the precious landscape of the Durham riverbanks has recently been set out in a Management Plan, an important partnership agreement between owners and local authorities. The enhancement of the riverbanks as a suitable setting for the cathedral and castle was a recurrent preoccupation of the eighteenth-and nineteenth-century landscape improvers. In the twentieth century the emphasis was on the protection of that setting, not just in the environs of the river but across the wider landscape of the city's bowl. The 'great views' of the castle and cathedral are afforded special protection in the City Council's environmental and conservation policies, and serve to emphasise the inseparable relationship between Durham's buildings and landscape.

Finally it is worth noting that not all the parks and gardens of the city are the creations of corporate institutions. Dr and Mrs Hawgood during the 1980s and early 1990s replanted the grounds of Crook Hall in the cottage garden tradition, but with the richness and invention of the painter's eye; plantings included a Shakespeare Garden and a White Garden. New gardens have been added by the present owners, Keith and Maggie Bell. Set within the stone walls and earthworks of the restored medieval manor house with their fine views of the cathedral, they represent the continuity of landscape history in the city.

That continuity is also seen in the installation of 'The Way' on an exposed hillside adjoining the historic Wharton Park (1994). This is an abstract sculpture in Portland stone by Hamish Horsley, and was originally erected as 'Aion', spanning the River Team at the Gateshead Garden Festival in 1990. The City Council imaginatively contacted the Festival organisers to offer the sculpture a permanent home at Wharton Park, and it was moved here with generous partnership funding. Horsley found the new site inspiring and rearranged the sculpture to symbolise life's journey, reflecting too Cuthbert's journey to the peninsula. The sculpture took as its focus the distant view of the cathedral, set within great pylons of stone. In so doing 'The Way' maintained the landscape tradition that uses the cathedral as 'eye-catcher', framing views back to the peninsula from the surrounding parks and gardens, a tradition almost four hundred years old.

7

THE MODERN CITY

By 1860 the foundations of modern Durham were in place. Roads bypassed the city to the west and the railways arrived from three different directions to the edge of the town. New hospitals, penal and judicial buildings had all been built, while the growing civic power was recognised in the rebuilding of the Town Hall in the Market Place. On the peninsula the medieval citadel had been opened up and emasculated by the removal of its gates and fortifications. The castle had lost its bishop and gained the young university.

Late Victorian and Edwardian Durham

In the wider county beyond the city boundaries this period saw the continued expansion of the Durham coalfield, greatest between 1825 and 1880. The city landscape was not completely unaffected by this growth, with pits established in the Elvet area in 1815 and 1828, and later in the century at Aykley Heads, a colliery which fed the local gas works in Framwellgate. The Old Miners' Hall in North Road, headquarters of the Durham Miners Association, built in 1875 to the designs of T. Oliver of Newcastle upon Tyne, still retains much of its impressive façade despite later abuse. The Association quickly outgrew the building and, in 1913-15, H.T. Gradon's new Miners' Hall in Redhills Lane appeared in the best red brick Edwardian baroque.

Those industries particular to the city have also left their mark during this period. Carpet manufacture in Durham developed out of cloth weaving, an enterprise originally established by the corporation as early as 1614. After a lengthy history of failed ventures, Gilbert Henderson acquired the lease for a carpet manufactory in 1814 and the business steadily grew until 1903, when Henderson sold out to Crossley's of Halifax, who promptly closed the premises. Restarted by ex-employee Hugh Mackay, it remained on the Walkergate site until 1980 when all carpet production transferred to Dragonville, just outside the city centre. Within the great 'manufactory' that once stood on the Walkergate site there remained until recently one or two good Victorian buildings of note such as the Old Jute Store, designed by local architect C. Hodgson Fowler (*c.*1868-70). There is an equally strong tradition of organ building in Durham. In 1872, Harrison and Harrison moved into a former paper mill in Hawthorn Terrace and enlarged the premises. Their organ factory was still in operation there until its removal in recent years to Langley Moor. The original building has been sensitively converted to offices. In nearby Holly Street, Nelson's former organ factory is now a timber warehouse.

Alongside this industrial activity the commercial and retail trades were prospering too. In the Market Place a banking centre developed, Gibson's National Westminster Bank of 1876 being a most self-assured classical design. Barclays Bank across the road has one of Waterhouse's more modest Gothic façades, and the Lloyds Bank of around 1900 returns to the classical style. In the streets around the Market Place is an interesting collection of shop fronts: one of the oldest, of late eighteenth-century date, is at 43/44 Saddler Street. Victorian and Edwardian fronts of both classical (36 & 41/42 Saddler Street) and Gothic inspiration (68 Saddler Street, 22/23 Market Place) can still be seen. Gothic was of course the prevailing style for the Anglican and Roman Catholic churches in the nineteenth century. St Nicholas' Church in the Market Place has been mentioned earlier (chapter 4). Its elegance and orderliness contrasts sharply with E.R. Robson's bleak but distinctive St Cuthbert's, North Road (1858-63), with its later saddleback tower, and huge patterned slate roof that almost touches the ground. St Godric's (Roman Catholic) Church in Castle Chare commands a

72 *St Godric's Church of 1864, with its tower of 1909-10. Behind, the castle and cathedral on the peninsula.* Royston Thomas

73 *Old Shire Hall, Old Elvet was built in 1896-8 and extended in 1905. It now houses the University of Durham's administrative offices.* Royston Thomas

prominent position in the town and was designed by E.W. Pugin in 1864, also with a later tower, built without its intended spire (**72**).

Educational developments in the nineteenth century centred on the new university (see below). Anthony Salvin was employed as architect for their first buildings, and he was also retained for the relocation of Durham School from Palace Green to Quarryheads Lane in 1844. Salvin and George Pickering adapted an existing house, which was extended in 1853 and 1862. The site slowly developed into the group of fine stone buildings that stand today, with ranges by Sir Arthur Blomfield (1876 & 1889-1904), all now focussed on the hilltop chapel of 1924-6 (Brierley and Rutherford), crouched down low but all-seeing like a cat on a wall.

No survey of the Victorian period would be complete without that most intrusive but instructive building – Old Shire Hall (**73**). Designed by Barnes and Coates, it sits on one side of Old Elvet, big and baroque, quite out of scale with the rest of the street. Its red brick and terracotta has mellowed to a deep lustre so that in the post-Betjeman era it is highly regarded now as an old friend. It was not always so. Thomas Sharp, writing in 1937, called it 'one of the most grotesque buildings ever erected in a city with any claim to architectural distinction' and, in 1953, Nikolaus Pevsner said in a memorably damning comment that it was 'faced with that cursedly imperishable red Victorian brick, which is such crushing proof of technical proficiency and aesthetic dumbness'.

The growth of the city 1860–1940

In and around these major Victorian and Edwardian buildings, the city of Durham was growing, and its enlarged population needed housing. The appearance of new housing changed markedly in this period, and 1860 is a convenient, if approximate, watershed between the use of local materials and the gradual dominance of the ubiquitous red factory brick and Welsh slate, brought along the new rail network. Similarly smaller multi-paned sash windows were replaced by larger paned Victorian sashes with cheaply produced plate glass. These trends mark the final extinguishing of a vernacular building tradition in the city.

The growth in the town was never dramatic – there was no major industrial expansion to attract people to the town – but within its existing boundaries the city did have space to expand. The development on the rear of the town's burgage plots in the seventeenth and eighteenth centuries had never extended much beyond the peninsula, but proposals to build on the remaining plots in the mid- to late nineteenth century met with opposition from the Local Board of Health, who vetted and regulated building proposals. Only where plot amalgamation allowed adequate width for new streets was development allowed, for example Neville Street and Mavin Street.

The effect of this was to push house builders out to green field sites. The development form was invariably terraced and in the early nineteenth century, though new houses were provided with individual yards, there was no back lane provision. In the second half of the century these became the norm, though Colpitts Terrace (1856) is a rare example of a development with a common yard.

Up to 1920 the greatest expansion was on the west side of the city, close to the Great North Road and the Railway Station – Crossgate Peth, The Avenue, Western Hill, and so on. In the inter-war period, estates of predominantly semi-detached houses sprang up at Whinney Hill, North End and Gilesgate Moor. Sherburn Road estate was constructed in the 1930s to house the residents of Millburngate and Framwellgate – one of the major streets of the medieval town that had by the early years of this century largely degenerated into a multi-occupancy slum. The condition of such streets was symptomatic of the state of the town during the years of the Depression, reflecting the serious deprivation suffered by the coalfield communities that lay on the town's doorstep.

Thomas Sharp and 'Cathedral City – A Plan for Durham'

The 1930s witnessed a growing interest in our towns and cities and the need for their future development to be guided by comprehensive planning policies. The impact of the Second World War and the destruction by bombing of many cities only added a further, more urgent, impetus to this need. While some planners saw the creation of the new Garden Cities as the future, others, notably Thomas Sharp, strongly opposed the movement and instead advocated an urban renewal within our existing settlements and a return to the qualities of 'urban-ness' he so much admired in the English county town.

None was better known to Sharp than Durham. As a native of Bishop Auckland, he knew the city as a child but his professional contact with Durham was only established when he joined the North East Durham Joint Planning Committee in the mid-1930s. He soon attracted a national reputation within the profession through his polemical and often strident writings. In 1937, contributing to the best selling book *Britain and the Beast* he wrote of his county town:

> The city is small, and has the rather dirty and neglected air that seems inseparable from industrial blessings. But . . . it retains a beauty which would be precious anywhere but which amongst the crude mining camps of this county stands out like a flower amongst filth.

Sharp's text was a siren call to alert the city to three major developments. The first was the opportunity presented by the substantial programme of slum clearance then in progress. Next was the County Council's proposed demolition of much of Old Elvet and finally he warned against the same council's plan for a high level 'through road' across the neck of the peninsula.

The last two of these developments were halted by the outbreak of the Second World War and, with work in abeyance and the city surviving the worst of the German bombing campaign unscathed, the City Council appointed Sharp to 'prepare and submit an outline development plan and report'. This was presented in 1944.

In a wide-ranging plan Sharp began by endorsing the city's role as county town, administrative and retail centre, with very special educational, cultural and tourist potential. He proposed a limit on the town's population with new residential development directed to three areas on the edge of the settlement. Turning to the County Council's 'through road' proposals of 1931, he advocated a much lower, wider road that would pass under Claypath in a cutting, thereby keeping closer to the natural ground level along the riverbanks. The much-needed public buildings – shire hall, municipal offices, cultural buildings, car parks and bus station – would be located on sites adjacent to the new road (**74**).

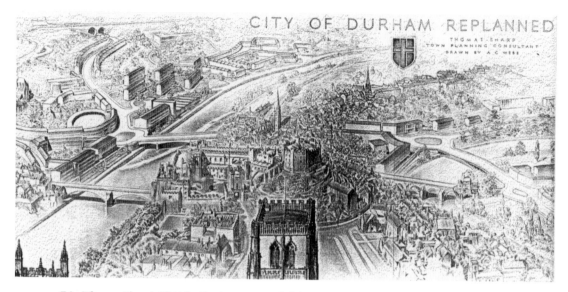

74 *Thomas Sharp's Plan for Durham proposed that the new road would serve major new developments in the city centre*

His report coincided with proposals for a large power station at Kepier, just north of the city, with chimneys 105m (350ft) high, cooling towers 75m (250ft) high and a turbine house 96 by 90 by 42m (320 by 300 by 140ft). The local authorities welcomed this immense project but Sharp reflected the views of a significant cross-section of local opinion when he concluded that to build it 'would be an act of blind and brutal philistinism'. The proposal was withdrawn and, in its wake, the orchestrated anger of local people was constructively channelled into a recently-formed amenity society, which became the forerunner of the present City of Durham Trust.

Sharp's report was written with passion and conviction. His descriptions of the Durham Coalfield pander to no political sensibilities and, in opposing the high level 'through road' and the power station, his opinion was influential. He drew significant conclusions on the topographical setting of the town and identified the importance of rooflines and the need to design buildings 'in the round', aware that in Durham they would be visible from several positions in the town. He stressed the need for new buildings to be 'true to their own time', yet the sketches he commissioned from the well-known architectural illustrator A.C. Webb showed poorly-articulated buildings, ill-fitting and insular, all set within a generous new road network. It all inevitably suffered by comparison with the richness and the urban complexity that Sharp himself had so eloquently described. This failure to illustrate a form of new development that responded to the historic context of Durham was criticised at the time in otherwise highly complimentary reviews.

Likewise his suggestion that upper Claypath and lower Gilesgate be cleared and turned into a natural park illustrates an attitude, common in the period, that often condemned historic urban vernacular in favour of an open vista or lawned setting of some greater monument. Despite these criticisms, in part viewed from our own perspective, Sharp's plan stood out amongst many produced after the war. It was applauded for its strong writing and its clear focus of balancing the desirability of preserving historic towns with the imperative for change to meet the demands of modern living. Sharp's report also examined the expansion of the university. He recommended that the 'through road' provided the best artery off which to develop five new colleges, south of Claypath and Gilesgate, facing the river. However, the future development of the university was, in the end, to be far greater than Sharp envisaged, and embraced a much larger sector of the city than anyone could then imagine.

The University of Durham

The growth and development of the university at Durham has been the greatest social and physical change that the city has had to accommodate in the last 150 years. Its growth during the nineteenth century was modest and, despite its broad foundation charter of 1832, teaching was almost exclusively theological in those early years. An exception was the study of astronomy, exemplified by Salvin's Observatory of 1840.

The new university was centred on the castle, later University College, and new halls of residence followed in 1846 at Bishop Hatfield's Hall (later college) and Bishop Cosin's Hall in 1851 (closed 1864). The structure of the university was collegiate, following the Oxbridge tradition. Women were admitted in 1895, taking their degrees through St Hild's College, one of three Colleges of Education in Durham. In parallel with the growth of the university, two private theological halls were founded in the Bailey: St Chad's (1904) and St John's (1909), both restyled as colleges in 1919.

The university during the nineteenth century was largely centred on the peninsula. Its gradual absorption of all the bishop's buildings, reinforced by the development of St Chad's and St John's Colleges, has ensured that the boundaries between the commercial town, the residential Bailey and the monastic/prebendal college remain almost as tightly defined as they were when stone walls and gates divided up the precincts of the medieval city. The hustle and bustle of Saddler Street shops ends at the steepest section of the street where the ramped passage of the great North Gate stood. Beyond it, there are only a couple of shop fronts on the peninsula and, behind the cathedral, the door still closes each evening beneath the College Gate to confine the dean and chapter in their monastic precincts – surely the happiest of those who find themselves nightly imprisoned in Durham!

Development on the present South Road site began with the first Science Laboratories in the Dawson Buildings in 1924. Science courses developed more strongly at Newcastle, where the university had firm links with the Medical School as early as 1852. In 1908 Durham University was reconstituted on a federal system with two (Durham and Newcastle) divisions, the latter known as King's College from 1937. In 1947 J.S. Allen's plan for the university proposed extensive demolition in the town to accommodate new buildings. This was abandoned in favour of more unobtrusive assimilation into the historic city, though Allen's West Buildings, a remnant of his development plan, were built in 1952 at South Road. On Allen's design team was the young (now Sir) William Whitfield, an architect whose influence on the city over the next forty years was to be considerable.

In 1963 the University of Newcastle upon Tyne was established in its own right and, at Durham, new buildings already under construction were supplemented by science buildings to compensate for those lost at Newcastle. The same year, when Old Shire Hall and many adjacent buildings in Old Elvet were vacated by the County Council, the university administration and several departments of the Faculty of Arts moved in. The developments in Elvet created a second centre for the university, divided by the River Wear. Ove Arup's Kingsgate Bridge (1962/3) elegantly united them, high above the river gorge. It was constructed in two halves parallel to the river, then turned and locked together. Though a modest commission by his standards, it was one that

75 *Dunelm House and Kingsgate Bridge.* Royston Thomas

Arup personally designed and cherished (**75**). Alongside the bridge Dunelm House, the Students Union building, was constructed 1961-5, designed by the Architects Co-Partnership. Uncompromisingly Brutalist in its style, it remains the best example in Durham of a building that makes no gestures towards slavish copying of the local vernacular yet evokes the city's fragmented building forms, tumbling riverside roofs, irregular fenestration and well-modelled pantiles in a wholly modern manner. The two structures, bridge and building, have been described as 'the greatest contribution modern architecture has made to the enjoyment of an English medieval city', and certainly the journey across the river to Bow Lane and the cathedral is memorable for its spatial and architectural contrasts.

The following year, the architects of Dunelm House designed Elvet Riverside lower down New Elvet (1962-6). It was planned to look inwards to a central pedestrian concourse running the length of much of New Elvet. The whole plan never materialised, leaving the building with its back to the street and no saving graces whatsoever. New building off the peninsula was concentrated to the south-east of the city, where the university estate included not only the Science Laboratories but also the well-landscaped and wooded nineteenth-century estates of Elvet Hill, Oswald House and Hollinside.

The Science Laboratories are generally a disappointing jumble of buildings responding, as they must, to the fluctuating demands of new teaching and research. Fortunately it is a well-contained disappointment as the margins of the site are generously planted and punctuated by one or two buildings of quality, such as Whitfield's Library of 1963-5. This, like many of his buildings in the region including the Psychology Building (1966-70) and Business School (1977-8) at Durham, is a stark, strongly articulated composition using his favourite dark brown brick and aggregate panels. Sir William Whitfield's great skill, evident in his buildings throughout the country, is his ability to reflect the prevailing regional building tradition in an entirely contemporary manner. It is a rare talent.

The expansion and improvement of the South Road site has continued in recent years with some utilitarian additions and more notably, down on South Road itself, the Chemistry building (1991 by Dewjoc Architects), imaginative and (sadly) largely hidden from public view. All too public in long distance views across the city is the School of Engineering (1987 by Faulkner-Brown), a fine building with strong reflective glazing – a condition best concealed in panoramas of the city.

Whitfield's South Road Library was science-based. The Arts Library on Palace Green was an enlargement by George Pace on a site critically positioned between castle and cathedral, perched over the river (**76**). It sits well and combines exposed concrete with 'Kentish Rag' masonry, alien to Durham but beautifully detailed and constructed. The South Road colleges reflect the growth of the university particularly during the 1960s. Only one, St Mary's, is

76 *University Library, Palace Green, constructed in 1961-6.* Royston Thomas

earlier (1952), designed by Vincent Harris, a monumental classical design spread out on the hillside opposite the peninsula, with strong Lutyens influences in evidence. St Aidan's (1962-4) is quite the opposite, a wholly contemporary building sited on the summit of Windmill Hill (**77**) and designed by Sir Basil Spence. Its dining room with great glazed walls and arched concrete roof reflects his more successful work at Sussex University but is still very impressive when viewed from its landscaped courtyard or from below. However, from the city centre, the skyline opportunity for dramatic silhouette is lost.

In all of the South Road colleges the integration of the landscape with the new buildings has been very successful, never more so than at Trevelyan (1964-7) by Stillman & Eastwick-Field, and Collingwood (1971-3) by Richard Shepherd Robson and partners. Both are economical, almost severe in their brown brick; the former organically generated as grouped polygons, the latter with arms radiating out and down to embrace the open landscape. The new college south of the Botanic Gardens, planned by the university in the last decade to the competition-winning design of Arup Associates, has begun with part of its residential accommodation let to the Graduate Society. The residential accommodation is designed in village clusters which, together with the communal buildings, will be ringed like a necklace around the base of a domed hill, from whose summit a panorama of the cathedral tower, another 'eye-catcher' view, can be obtained.

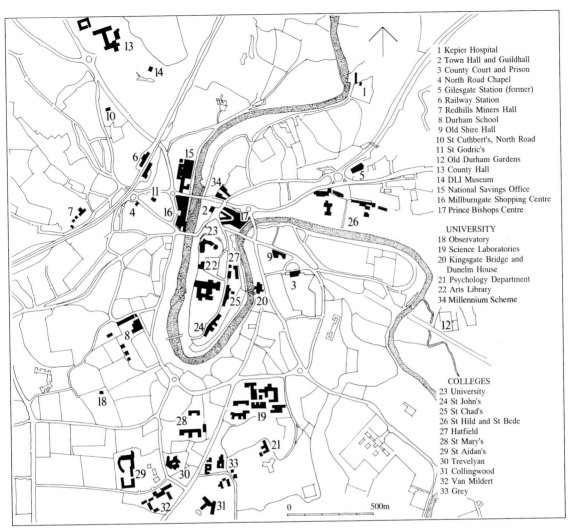

77 *Map of present-day Durham, identifying buildings mentioned in the text*

1 Kepier Hospital
2 Town Hall and Guildhall
3 County Court and Prison
4 North Road Chapel
5 Gilesgate Station (former)
6 Railway Station
7 Redhills Miners Hall
8 Durham School
9 Old Shire Hall
10 St Cuthbert's, North Road
11 St Godric's
12 Old Durham Gardens
13 County Hall
14 DLI Museum
15 National Savings Office
16 Millburngate Shopping Centre
17 Prince Bishops Centre

UNIVERSITY
18 Observatory
19 Science Laboratories
20 Kingsgate Bridge and
    Dunelm House
21 Psychology Department
22 Arts Library
34 Millennium Scheme

COLLEGES
23 University
24 St John's
25 St Chad's
26 St Hild and St Bede
27 Hatfield
28 St Mary's
29 St Aidan's
30 Trevelyan
31 Collingwood
32 Van Mildert
33 Grey

0   500m

Durham 1945-2002

The Second World War, and the period of austerity that followed it, greatly delayed the implementation of the County Council's new 'through road' and the plans to move its headquarters to Aykley Heads to the north-west of the city centre, rather than redevelop Old Elvet. Their transfer to the new County Hall had to wait until 1963. The new building, its out-moded design demonstrating its long gestation, sits on the edge of the Durham bowl. If its blockish prominence on the city's skyline seems unfortunate, it should be remembered that a ten-storey tower was originally planned.

Nearby, and much more of its time, the Durham Light Infantry Museum and Art Gallery (1964-8) by Tarren and Caller was a beautifully simple design, superbly set in a reclaimed colliery tip. The past tense is regrettably appropriate here, for recent enlargements have totally destroyed the fine balance between solid and void, rendering it less a piece of good architecture, more a box for museum exhibits.

In the city centre, Sharp's influence on the 'through road' kept it low, avoiding the junction with Claypath and the construction of huge embankments. But his proposal to have no direct links with Claypath was ignored and two slip roads were eventually added, thereby widening the gap between the Market Place and the severed limb of Claypath. The bridging of that gap with buildings to restore the townscape continuity was to become the 'holy grail' of the City Council for the following thirty years.

The 'through road' (1967-75) was built in two stages, first from North Road to Gilesgate via Millburngate Bridge, then the route across to Elvet via New Elvet Bridge. The construction of the road, coupled with adjacent cleared land, released the large area of the city centre for development that Sharp had envisaged. These major development sites posed the perennial question of how to assimilate large-scale modern developments into the fabric of a small historic town – a fabric with a dominant focal point of the cathedral and castle which, by common acclaim, must never be challenged.

Such orthodoxies did not upset the vanities of those designers who saw in *their* development a building worthy of overshadowing the cathedral. The lessons of the Kepier power station and the County Hall tower block had clearly not been learnt by those responsible for the establishment of part of the National Savings Office in Durham in 1961. The first design was for a thirteen-storey point block, and only after much local and national consultation was the building redesigned in its present form (1965-9). The two thousand jobs it brought with it were much needed in Durham at a time when mines were closing all around. The building itself makes absolutely no concession to the character of the city or to the river along which it lies. It is a poor compliment that the best that can be said of it is that it could have been worse. The City Council at this time, through its officers and consultant architect-planners, Thomas Sharp and later William Whitfield, were in close liaison with the County Council's Planning Department on a wide range of issues to do with the city, and policies were formulated for its protection. In 1968 the Durham Conservation Area was designated and in 1980 it was greatly enlarged.

In 1974 the new City of Durham Council appointed its own City Planning Officer, Tony Scott, with a full complement of planning and conservation staff. The Council at its first meeting approved the major Policy for the Protection of the Architectural Heritage of the City of Durham, which reflected much of the County Council's earlier wisdom on planning control and laid down for the first time specific criteria against which all new development must be judged. These included the importance of views into and out of the town; the

78 *Millburngate Shopping Centre. The first phase, in the foreground, was built 1974-6. The second phase, beyond the trees, followed in 1984-7.* Graeme Stearman

need for fragmentation of built forms, ensuring the complexities of rooflines, and the choice of appropriate materials.

Much of this advice had earlier been incorporated into the development brief, first drafted by Whitfield, for the initial phase of Millburngate Shopping Centre. This was designed by the Building Design Partnership, who skilfully articulated a large mass of retail development so that it was assimilated into the urban fabric of the town (**78**). Its second phase by the same architects is broadly similar, with contemporary fashion points such as its glazed atrium and cast iron pavilion. Its difficulty lay in more than doubling the mass of the centre, making the whole a little indigestible. However, it enclosed the Millburngate bridgehead neatly and gave Durham another surprise view.

William Whitfield's Cathedral (formerly Leazes Bowl) Car Park (1975) was perhaps even more successful within the difficult design constraints that a car park imposes (**79**). Its battered and buttressed walls, pierced by slender stair turrets, echoed the defensive wall that once girded the town at this point. In case the metaphor was lost on some observers, Whitfield humorously offered the toilet stair block adjacent to Elvet Bridge as a more authentic looking medieval tower. Ironically the tower survived but the car park did not. Sitting on an important city centre site and plagued by awkward circulation, a bleak interior and high repair costs, its future was never that bright. Perhaps that is as it should be. Inert and dehumanising, car parks are best kept away from public view. Yet Leazes Bowl remained externally one of the best-designed car parks in the country; the sadness in its loss lies in the monster that replaced it.

Alongside these major developments, the City Council seized the opportunities created by the removal of through traffic from the medieval streets to

173

79 *Cathedral Car Park (1974-5), centre and right foreground, in its urban context. The building was demolished in the mid-1990s to make way for the Prince Bishops Shopping Centre.* Royston Thomas

push ahead with the Pedestrianisation and Floorscaping Schemes of the City Centre (1975-7). From this stemmed new controls on shop fronts and advertising. In the atmosphere of regeneration thus created, a number of the town centre shops extended and enlarged. Those to the rear of Silver Street and the Market Place demonstrate not only individual design skills, e.g. WHSmith's by Simons Design (1980), but Sharp's truism that Durham streets rarely have a rear that cannot be viewed from some other place.

Beside these commercial developments, new housing at Briardene (1972-8) by Donald Insall and Associates and South Street (1976-8) by Gazzard and Burns are noteworthy. In 1986 the quality of the city's unique architectural heritage was recognised by the inscription by UNESCO of the castle and cathedral as a World Heritage Site. The impact of the through road has continued to be the decisive physical influence upon the city centre of the late twentieth and the early years of the twenty-first centuries. While much of the development of the centre of Durham must be conservation-led, so nationally and internationally important are the buildings and landscapes it contains, those sites which were first cleared over forty years ago for the construction of the new road still present the best opportunity for the larger scale developments that need to enrich and energise the modern city. The zone around the new road, free of historic constraints, may over a long period emerge as an area where buildings are recycled as priorities change. While some sites still remain undeveloped, the Paradise Gardens site, first occupied by Leazes Bowl Car Park, is now host to the Prince Bishops Shopping Centre (Benoy, 1998).

The Prince Bishops meets the demands for extra shopping development in the heart of the city and has shifted the retail centre of gravity away from Millburngate. The Centre may well have stimulated economic growth but the damaging physical impact of the building inevitably raises questions of whether the much-needed investment could have been achieved in a different and far more sophisticated form. To be fair, the development is a very mixed bag. Its open streets are very welcome, employing traditional materials and variable frontages on gently weaving building lines – all a bit whimsical but far better than rigid glass-roofed 'anytown' shopping. Two streets start at the Market Place and Saddler Street with tidy corner designs, then snake away to meet at an anonymous little place, that should have been so much better. And that is it. In a city whose every historic road, lane and vennel invites exploration, these streets go nowhere. What should be living twenty-four hour city streets only vibrate with life for less than half the day.

The centre is a single level of shopping set on top of a multi-storey car park. It sits on ground that slopes swiftly down to the flood plain of the river. Denying the fall of the natural topography creates a riverside elevation of monstrous proportions – a Herculean task for any designer to assimilate into the city. Attempts to fragment the elevation fail disastrously and the only new articulated focal point, the staircase, receives the most offensive green-glazed brick cladding – a hard acid green totally lacking empathy with the colour and texture of Durham walls. The public and professional criticism of the Prince Bishops' Centre was severe and remained a constant presence during the gestation of the city's next major development – the Millennium Scheme.

The Millennium Scheme, conceived and managed by the City Council, grew from a number of issues in the town. There was an outstanding requirement for further major car parking. Well-used amenities such as libraries and cinemas were occupying inadequate buildings in the town. The city wanted to expand its facilities for receiving tourists and visitors. Finally it needed a cultural focus, an auditorium and multi-purpose hall, that could host music and theatre as well as serve as a major centre for the city's expanding conference business. The brief for the development of vacant and derelict land at Claypath and Freemans Place envisaged what in effect would be a new cultural quarter for the city. It included on Claypath a multi-purpose hall, library, community resource centres, tourist information and visitor centres which were to be linked to commercially funded multi-screen cinema and other leisure activities on the lower Freemans Place site, known later as the Walkergate development.

The site was an interesting one – with Framwellgate Peth it was the last large 'post-through road' site to be developed. Historically the Henderson-Mackay carpet factory had dug deep into the lower half of the sloping

80 *Millennium Place (2001).* Royston Thomas

ground, resulting in a stepped site so severe that no access was possible between the two halves. This created the opportunity for burying below the natural slope line most of the large-scale elements of the brief that required no natural light, of which cinemas and car parks were an obvious choice. It was regrettable, but probably unavoidable, that the last of the stone carpet factory buildings, unlisted and set deep within their site, were removed for the scheme (**80**). A design competition was won by the distinguished London architects, MacCormac Jamieson Prichard (MJP), and the City Council was awarded generous Millennium Commission lottery funding to help implement the scheme.

Taking the Claypath corner as the entrance to the development, architect David Prichard designed a radiating layout around a central new public space, using the geometry of the library and multi-purpose hall to thrust outwards over terraces stepping down towards the river. The design introduced public access into the site for the first time in its history – radially down through the restored slope of cascading buildings and laterally across the contours to link with the slip road and invite future links to the north, behind Claypath. Those links through the lower Walkergate development have been temporarily delayed by the shifting economic sands of the leisure industry. So, for now, the upper Millennium Scheme stands artificially high on its retaining walls awaiting the pedestrian routes to be fully realised.

The completed scheme now balances the Gala Theatre and Clayport Library around the new Millennium Place, both buildings well-christened with local names that help root them to their site. The architectural design is unashamedly contemporary and, as appropriate for buildings of iconic stature in Durham, both theatre and library are clad predominantly in stone where displays of glass are not called for. Their supporting buildings are more modestly rendered. The Clayport Library, with its raking roof, screens the square from the road and its monolithic walls, minimally pierced and slashed for light, send a powerful, and a very Durham, message across the river. To the square it remains strong, its stone walls cut away completely at ground level to reveal the activity of the library within.

The much larger Gala Theatre opposite builds from the radiating theatre form, starting with the bold red-painted box of the auditorium, its roof echoing that of the library, all lines diverging in both plan and elevation. Around the auditorium the open glazed public areas are held in check by the oversailing roof and by two great stone staircases, giving strong visual support. The larger southern tower, seen from the entrance to the square, leads the eye towards the theatre foyer. This is a dynamic and exciting building, its large glazing well controlled, if rather over assertively lit at night – glass in quantity will always be a problem in Durham. Only the ruthless logic of its red auditorium roof jars in distant panoramas of the city, bringing to mind Alec Clifton-Taylor's remark that 'at Durham, nothing, absolutely and positively nothing, must ever be permitted to intrude upon the great views'.

This entire development is designed with concern for detail and MJP's characteristic articulation of building elements – wall, roof, windows, etc. all seemingly frozen at the moment of explosive separation – is beautifully handled. The Millennium Scheme has re-established faith in both Durham's ability to enlarge its architectural heritage with public buildings of real quality, and the ability of modern architects to integrate their buildings into the fabric of the historic town. Most successfully, it has given the city the cultural heart it so badly needed.

The Walkergate development will follow, hopefully, along the design principles already established – gently descending buildings, linked by a web of inviting spaces, generous steps and new vennels to explore, all less monumental in scale and materials than the Millennium Place, providing for it an appropriate setting. The large car park, when built, will finally have found its true home in Durham – completely hidden from view.

The Millennium Scheme has brought about development on a number of vacant Council-owned sites in the city centre. The recently opened Penny Ferry Bridge (Mott McDonald 2001) links the Millennium Square-Walkergate sites to Framwellgate Waterside where a new hotel is proposed. Of the Council-owned sites, only two are under construction at the time of writing. On the small plot below St Margaret's Church in South Street now stands a small housing scheme that has neatly restored the more vernacular townscape to that damaged junction. On Framwellgate Peth a far more ambitious and, in its own way, controversial, housing development is in progress. The scheme (RPS Clouston – architects) looks backwards with a well-detailed replication of the Georgian Durham town house, devised around a challenging terraced site – a development one esteemed commentator said might just work, architecturally speaking, provided there were 'no false notes'. Final judgement on this must await completion.

A TOUR OF THE CITY

In his *Handbook to the Roman Wall* (1863), Collingwood Bruce wrote a memorable preface. He hoped his book would be 'travelling with its owner and sharing his fortunes of wind and weather . . . honourably scarred and stained . . .'. Although it is not the primary purpose of this volume that it be carried around as a guidebook, it may, nevertheless, be helpful to suggest a walk that incorporates the major buildings and viewpoints of the city described in these pages.

What I hope such a walk may also do is enable the visitor to experience the contrasts in Durham: between the built and the natural environment; a sense of activity and one of tranquillity; feelings of openness and containment, height and depth. The path, therefore, is not always straight or level and the walk may take an hour if you keep moving, or a whole day if you wish to stop and explore.

Start in Millennium Place, where a visit to the Tourist Information Centre and the Visitor Centre will enable you to confirm the opening times of the major historic buildings on and around the peninsula (current times listed below), and see the new film on the life of St Cuthbert. Cross to the Market Place, then up Saddler Street, branching only to visit the vennels of Saddlers Yard on your right. Continue on to Owengate and Palace Green, where the castle and cathedral invite inspection. After your visits, pass through the church into the cloisters and the dormitory on its south side. Go out into the College, then right into Dark Entry to emerge onto a terrace above the river. Drop down to the riverbanks, then back to the Water Gate and along South Bailey to the Heritage Centre at St Mary-le-Bow, where the history of the city is richly displayed.

Proceed down Bow Lane and across Kingsgate Bridge to Dunelm House for a view of modern Durham, then south along Church Street. Branch off to the right, across the beautiful churchyard of St Oswald's, to the path above the Wear, that as it drops, is absorbed into the woodland of the riverbanks. Skirt the southern tip of the peninsula to the west end of Prebends Bridge, then up the path to South Street, where in summer months the unforgettable view of the peninsula is gradually revealed through the foliage. Return via Framwellgate Bridge, up Silver Street to the Town Hall and Guildhall in the Market Place.

For those with a little more time, a walk out to one of the vantage points overlooking the city centre would be worthwhile. Wharton Park, above the railway station, provides one of the classic panoramas. Further east, the views from Pelaw Woods and Old Durham Gardens are superb. Whinney Hill, to the south-east of the city centre, is something of a hidden treasure, as the paths are not easy to find. Finding them brings the visitor, in his exploration of Durham, to the point from which I started, and the point at which I must end.

Opening Times

Castle: Guided tours only (45 minutes). Tours take place on most days out of term, and each day from Easter to 30th September. For other periods, tours are on Monday, Wednesday and Saturday and Sunday afternoons. Other events sometimes result in cancellation of tours. It is therefore advisable to check with the Castle Porter (on 0191 374 3800) before arrival. www.durhamcastle.com

Cathedral: Open for worship and prayer on Sundays between 7.45am and 12.30pm and from Monday to Saturday from 7.30-9.30am. Also open for visitors until 5.00pm on Sunday and until 6.15pm from Monday–Saturday. During the summer from 17th June to 8th September the Cathedral remains open until 8.00pm. A number of the claustral buildings are usually also accessible to visitors for exhibitions and by virtue of use, including refectory undercroft, dormitory, dormitory undercroft (Treasury and restaurant) and priory kitchen (bookshop). For details phone 0191 386 4266. www.durhamcathedral.co.uk

Old Fulling Mill Archaeological Museum: November to March, Friday through to Monday, 11.30am-3.30pm. April to October, daily, 11.00am-4.30pm.

St Mary-le-Bow Heritage Centre: April to October: April and May weekends and Bank Holidays, 2.00-4.30pm, June to October, daily, 2.00-4.30pm. July and August, daily 11.00am-4.30pm. Also groups by appointment.

Town Hall and Guildhall: Open weekdays throughout the year, access may be limited by civic or other function.

Old Durham Gardens: The lower garden is accessible at all times from the riverside footpath.

(N.B. Visitors are advised to check all times of opening at the Tourist Information Centre in Millennium Place, where details of the Visitor Centre film about the life of St Cuthbert – 'Sacred Journey' – can also be obtained.) www.durhamcity.gov.uk

THE BISHOPS OF DURHAM

From the Norman Conquest to 1836

Aethelwin	1056–1071	Richard Fox	1494–1501
Walcher	1071–1080	William Sever	1502–1505
William of St Calais	1081–1096	Christopher Bainbridge	1507–1508
Rannulph Flambard	1099–1128	Thomas Ruthall	1509–1523
Geoffrey Rufus	1133–1141	Thomas Wolsey	1523–1529
William of St Barbara	1143–1152	Cuthbert Tunstall	1530–1559
Hugh of Le Puiset	1153–1195	James Pilkington	1561–1576
Philip of Poitou	1197–1208	Richard Barnes	1577–1587
Richard Marsh	1217–1226	Matthew Hutton	1589–1595
Richard Poore	1228–1237	Tobias Matthew	1595–1606
Nicholas Farnham	1241–1249	William James	1606–1617
Walter Kirkham	1249–1260	Richard Neile	1617–1627
Robert Stichill	1261–1274	George Monteigne	1628
Robert of Holy Island	1274–1283	John Howson	1628–1632
Anthony Bek	1284–1311	Thomas Morton	1632–1659
Richard Kellaw	1311–1316	John Cosin	1660–1672
Lewis de Beaumont	1318–1333	Nathaniel Crewe	1674–1722
Richard of Bury	1333–1345	William Talbot	1722–1730
Thomas Hatfield	1345–1381	Edward Chandler	1730–1750
John Fordham	1382–1388	Joseph Butler	1750–1752
Walter Skirlaw	1388–1406	Richard Trevor	1752–1771
Thomas Langley	1406–1437	John Egerton	1771–1787
Robert Neville	1438–1457	Thomas Thurlow	1787–1791
Laurence Booth	1457–1476	The Hon Shute	
William Dudley	1476–1483	Barrington	1791–1826
John Shirwood	1485–1494	William Van Mildert	1826–1836

FURTHER READING

Space does not permit referenced notes, nor an exhaustive bibliography. For those who wish to check my sources, a fully referenced manuscript copy of the book will be lodged with Durham County Record Office. What I have attempted to do below is set out some of the books etc. that have helped me most, in supplementing my own researches, and which the reader may wish to consult for further study. I have attached notes where relevant.

General

Clack, P., *The Book of Durham City*, Barracuda, 1985

Dewdney, J.C. (ed.), *Durham County and City with Teesside*, British Association, 1970

Lomas, R., *North-East England in the Middle Ages,* John Donald, 1992

Lowther, P. *et al.*, 'The City of Durham: An Archaeological Survey', *Durham Archaeological Journal, 9,* 1993

Page, W. (ed.), *Victoria County History: Durham*, 3 volumes, London, 1905-28

Pevsner, N. & Williamson E., *Buildings of England: County Durham*, 2nd edition, Penguin Books, 1983

Surtees, R., *The history and antiquities of the County palatine of Durham,* 4 volumes, London, 1816-40

The castle

Johnson M., 'The Great North Gate of Durham Castle', *Transactions of the Architectural and Archaeological Society of Durham and Northumberland,* 4, 1978

Jones, W. T., 'The walls and towers of Durham'. *Durham University Journal*, 22-3, 1920-3, 6 parts

These two detailed papers supplement the thorough VCH account (1928), the last major published work on the castle.

Rollason, D., Harvey, M. & Prestwich M. (eds), *Anglo-Norman Durham 1093-1193,* Boydell Press, 1994

A major publication on the history, archaeology and architecture of Norman Durham. There are several papers of importance on both the castle and cathedral as well as illuminating accounts of the great builder-bishops of the period.

The cathedral

Cramp, R. *et al.*, *Medieval Art and Architecture at Durham Cathedral*, British Archaeological Association, 1980

Dobson, R. B., *Durham Priory 1400-1450*, Cambridge University Press, Cambridge, 1973

Stranks, C. J., *This Sumptuous Church: The story of Durham Cathedral*, SPCK, London, 1973

Fowler J. T. (ed.), 'Rites of Durham' (1593), *Surtees Society*, Volume CV111, 1903

Fowler J. T. (ed.), 'Account rolls of the abbey of Durham', *Surtees Society*, Volume XCIX, C, CIII, 1898, 1900

Extracts in Latin, but a rich source of documentary material.

McAleer, P., 'The North Portal of Durham Cathedral and the problem of 'Sanctuary' in Medieval Britain', *The Antiquaries Journal*, 81, 2001

The medieval town

Bonney, M., *Lordship and the urban community: Durham and its overlords, 1250-1540*, Cambridge University Press, Cambridge, 1990

A solitary, but very important, book on the subject of the medieval town. Extensive documentary research into the priory archives.

Durham 1550-1860

Johnson, M.(ed.), *John Cosin: From Priest to Prince Bishop*, Turnstone Ventures, 1997

Parks and gardens

There has been little published material on the subject. The Cosin Correspondence and Durham Account Rolls (see above) have valuable references.

Allen, A. & Roberts, M., 'Excavations at Old Durham Gardens, Durham City, 1989-92', *Durham Archaeological Journal*, 10, 1994

The modern city

Sharp, T., *Cathedral City: A Plan For Durham*, Architectural Press, London, 1945

GLOSSARY

almoner: the monk of the priory responsible for the poor and infirm, including the administration of two almshouses, two hospitals and a school.

arch:

basket arch: a three-centred arch with a single segmented arch in the centre, resembling the handle of a basket.

four-centred arch: a depressed, pointed arch composed of two pairs of arcs, the lower pair drawn from two centres on the springing line and the upper pair from centres below the springing line.

baldachin: a ceremonial canopy over an altar or tomb, usually supported on columns.

battery: a fortified emplacement for heavy guns.

bine twist: the stem of a climbing plant that spirals as it grows, formalised in architectural decoration.

bolection moulding: a convex moulding which projects beyond the surface it frames, common in seventeenth- and early eighteenth-century joinery.

burgage plots: the medieval division of land in the town. The plots in Durham were usually long and narrow, end on to the street.

cellarer: the monk responsible for acquiring food and drink for the kitchen of the priory.

claustral: belonging to the cloisters of a church as in the ranges that surround the cloister walk.

clerestory: the upper storey of the nave above the aisle roofs, pierced with windows to illuminate the interior.

feretory: the space in a church where a saint's shrine is kept.

finials and drops: the ornaments that crown the top and protrude from the bottom of a stair newel.

fleche: a slender spire, often perforated with windows or open tracery.

gablets: a small gable, often used ornamentally on buttresses, over niches, etc. but at Durham employed on a larger scale over the gallery.

garderobe: a medieval privy.

hostillar: the monk responsible for the accommodation and entertainment of guests in the priory.

lancet: a narrow, pointed arch whose span is shorter than its radius.

laver: a washing place, normally found in the cloister, equipped with a piped water supply.

lunettes: a semi-circular window or panel.

newel: the principal post at the angles of a square staircase.

obedientaries: monks who were in charge of the various administrative departments of the priory.

ogee: a pointed arch, formed by two convex arcs above and two concave ones below.

Palatinate: the territory, principally in County Durham and north Northumberland, under the secular control of the bishops of Durham, originating as the lands of the Anglo-Saxon Community of St Cuthbert. Within his Palatinate, the bishop enjoyed royal privilege and status, being able to enforce legislation, control the courts and mint his own coinage. His powers were greatly reduced by Henry VIII and finally abolished in 1836.

parterre: a flat terrace usually adjacent to the house and laid out with flowers or other decorative patterns, to be seen from above.

paterae: circular or oval disc-like classical ornaments.

reredorter: medieval latrines in a monastery (literally 'behind the dormitory').

revestry: in Durham, the sixteenth-century name for the building beside the south choir aisle of the cathedral, used exclusively by the bishop for the occasional ordination of priests and other episcopal duties, so as not to interfere with the monastic use of the choir and high altar.

slype: covered way or passage, especially that between the transept and chapter house in the east range of the cloisters.

spandrel: the triangular area contained by one side of an arch and the horizontal and vertical lines that define the rectangular frame around it.

squinches: the small arches built across the angles of a tower to receive an octagonal spire or dome.

strings: two sloping members which carry the ends and treads of a staircase. Closed strings enclose the treads and rises: in the later open string staircase, the steps project above the strings.

tree-ring dating: the dating of old timbers by the detailed study of their annual growth rings which can establish a very close date for the felling of the tree used.

triforium: the horizontal division of a church above the arcade but below the aisle roofs and the clerestory. Often only a wall passage, at Durham Cathedral it is a full aisle-wide gallery.

truncated principal roof: a regionally distinctive roof structure of broadly late medieval to seventeenth-century date, in which the principal rafters of the trusses do not rise to the ridge, but are cut short and braced by a horizontal collar that supports the upper purlins.

vault:

tunnel vault: an uninterrupted vault of semi-circular section.

groin vault: a type of vaulting taking its name from the arched diagonals or groins formed by the intersection of two tunnel vaults at right angles.

rib vault: a system of vaulting of which the groins are replaced by arched ribs constructed across the sides and diagonals of the vaulting bay.

quadripartite vault: a rib vault in which each bay is divided by two diagonal ribs into four compartments.

voussoirs: the wedge-shaped stones used to form an arch.

INDEX

References in **bold** denote figure numbers